ESPRESSO
Ultimate Coffee

Kenneth Davids

COLE
GROUP

President and Publisher   Brete C. Harrison
VP and Director of Operations   Linda Hauck
VP of Publishing   Robert G. Manley
VP Marketing and Business Development   John A. Morris
VP and Editorial Director   James Connolly
Director of Production   Steve Lux
Art Editor and Production Assistant   Dotti Hydue
Senior Editor   Annette Gooch
Editorial Assistants   Penny Hastings; Susanne Fitzpatrick
Design   Octavo; Steve Lux
Production   Octavo
Cover Photography   Paul Schulz
Illustrations   Michael Surles; Octavo

Distributed to the book trade by Publishers Group West

Printed and bound in Hong Kong through Mandarin Offset

Published by Cole Group, Inc.
1330 N. Dutton Ave., #103
Santa Rosa, CA 95401
(800) 959-2717
(707) 526-2682
FAX (707) 526-2687

B	C	D	E	F	G	H
5	6	7	8	9	0	1

Library of Congress Catalog Card Number 92-3283 /

ISBN 1-56426-557-9

CONTENTS

ESPRESSO AND ME

I realized that espresso cuisine had finally truly arrived in America when Dave's Coffee Shop in Oakland, California, situated across the street from two automobile dealers and next to a technical high school, put up a large yellow sign indicating that it too, along with every other place in town, finally served "Espresso" (spelled correctly, with an s), thus assuring the nearby automobile salesmen and high school students, not to mention motorists on the long, dry run between caffès in downtown Oakland and Berkeley, that they need no longer be deprived of their cappuccino or "latte."

This is a book that attempts to demystify espresso, in all of its varied incarnations, from the purist's short pull of straight espresso to the shopping mall cuisine of chocolate-almond caffè lattes and the triple cappuccinos nursed by college students preparing for all-night study sessions. Espresso cuisine is mysterious, not only because it is produced by large, complex machines that make locomotive-like noises but also because it is an alternative coffee tradition to the American cuisine of medium-roasted, light-bodied filter coffee. And because it is a different tradition, it brings with it other culinary procedures, other institutions, other rituals. It means caffès, bars, and carts instead of coffee shops and diners; small, perfumy cups of dark coffee and frothy cappuccinos rather than bottomless cups from coffee urns or drip brewers.

In the following pages I've tried to respond to most of the questions one might ask about espresso: questions about its technical aspects, its history, its mythology, its culture, and above all, how to do whatever one wants to do with it at home. I've attempted to give clear and complete advice about all aspects of producing good home espresso cuisine, while adding enough espresso history, fact, and myth to bring the procedures to life.

The Espresso Generation

My own involvement with espresso, at least in what might be called a professional sense, goes back to the time in my life when I nursed a cranky old Cimbali espresso machine in a caffè I co-owned and managed in Berkeley, California. Subsequently I sold the caffè and wrote a book on coffee, which is now in its fourth edition: *Coffee: A Guide to Buying, Brewing, and Enjoying*. But espresso was not an afterthought in my personal coffee history; in fact, it started my coffee history. Since my experience is in many ways typical of my generation of coffee drinkers, it might be worth briefly pursuing.

Like many Americans who came of age in the late 1950s and early 1960s, I did not grow up drinking coffee. The only pressing choice I faced was whether to drink Pepsi or Coca-Cola. Coffee was some sour brown stuff drunk for unknown reasons by people over thirty, presumably while they occupied themselves with other peculiar middle-aged activities, like watching Ed Sullivan, listening to Frank Sinatra, and petting their cocker spaniels.

The first inkling I had that there might be something worthwhile to the stuff was during my first college-student trip to Europe. While hitchhiking from France to Italy, I was picked up by a ruddy-faced Italian doctor. As soon as we reached the Italian side of the border, he turned, squinted at me, drew himself up, and intoned grandly: "Do you like *coffee*?" The well-traveled reader will understand the length and sonorous authority of the vowel sounds involved in that question.

I responded that I wasn't sure. Whereupon he literally skidded to a stop in front of the next espresso bar (actually the first espresso bar, since we had just entered Italy), strode up to the gleaming counter, ordered two espressos, dumped three or four spoonfuls of sugar in his, muddled them, and drank the results, all in about the time that it took me to follow him in from the car.

I didn't much care for that first dark little cup, but

somewhere between Genoa and Florence I learned, like most Americans do, to order a cappuccino, and from there progressed and regressed through the rest of the carefully modulated drinks of the espresso cuisine, from milky *latte macchiato* to the *corto espresso*, with barely enough rich, heavy, creamy espresso to cover the bottom of a demitasse. Along the way I learned to stand properly with one elbow on the bar, stare at the passing Fiats while downing my espresso drink in several swallows, then replace the cup on the saucer with the proper authoritative clack. Above all I learned to love the peculiar bittersweet richness of espresso drinks, which rings on one's tastebuds like a delicious, dark bellclap, a sort of musical accompaniment to the lingering resonance of the caffeine.

On my return to the United States I discovered the Italian-American caffè, that more leisurely, spacious throwback to an Italy before the advent of the espresso bar, and began to drink my cappuccinos in places like the Caffè Reggio in Manhattan, the Caffè Mediterraneum in Berkeley, and the Caffè Trieste in San Francisco. Caffès became my true home, and since in those days most of them were across the street from a bookstore, I had everything I needed in life clustered around my temporarily rented marbletop table: books, newspapers, espresso coffee, sympathetic friends, plus an occasional sandwich. I recall spending long, fruitless hours in towns without either Italians or caffès, driving around looking for a proper cappuccino and a proper place to drink it. When I taught at the University of Hawaii for a year, I ended up learning not only to make my own cappuccino, but roast my own coffee as well, since in those years

there did not appear to be a single dark-roasted coffee bean on the entire island of Oahu, aside from the ones I roasted myself in a frying pan in the oven of my tin-roofed bungalow in Kaneohe.

Given that history, it was inevitable that I would be drawn to opening my own caffè, which I eventually did, and writing a book on coffee, which I also did. In the fifteen years since I sold the caffè and published the first edition of *Coffee: A Guide to Buying, Brewing and Enjoying,* I have nursed the idea of writing a second coffee book, a book on espresso alone. Finally, with mini espresso machines inundating the gourmet sections of department stores, and drive-by espresso stands and espresso carts outside every grocery store and half the gas stations in some West Coast cities, a publisher finally has taken me up on the offer. I hope this book is as gratifying to read as it was to write, and above all, to research.

Espresso Thanks

In the course of that writing and research I have run up an enormous collective debt to those involved in the art and business of coffee and espresso.

My thanks first to those manufacturers and distributors who gave or lent me equipment, including Braun, Krups, Saeco, Thomas Cara, The Coffee Beanery, and Windward Trading, and to those individuals and businesses, particularly the Victoria Arduino company, the publishers of William Ukers' *All About Coffee*, and BE-MA Editrice, publishers of Ambrogio Fumagalli's *Macchine da Caffè,* for permitting Cole Group and me to make use of illustrations from their publications.

When I turn from businesses to individuals the list of those to whom I am indebted grows much longer.

I would like to particularly thank Bob Barker, who read through the entire typescript and made many valuable suggestions; Christopher and John Cara of Thomas Cara, Ltd.; Chuck Beek of Seattle; David Schomer of Espresso Vivace in Seattle; collector Ambrogio Fumagalli of Milan; Erik Kooijmans of Saeco in Italy; Danielle Giovannucci, of Fante's in Philadelphia; and Australian collector, coffee-man, and writer Ian Bersten. I am also in debt to Charles Pomeroy and Scott Anderson of Caffè Acorto; Al Avolicino of Ameritalia; Chris Bonk of TMR, San Francisco; Ben Leuenberger of MADAG, Switzerland; Roger Sandon and Carole Paulson of *Café Olé* magazine; and Daryl Ross of Caffè Strada, Berkeley.

To those individuals I would add the many others who assisted me in the research for the several editions of my previous book, including its British version.

I consulted the books of many others during the course of assembling this one, in particular Ambrogio Fumagalli's *Macchine da Caffè*; Ian Bersten's brilliantly researched *Coffee Floats, Tea Sinks*; Edward and Joan Bramah's *Coffee Makers, 300 Years of Art & Design*; Francesco and Riccardo Illy's *Coffee to Espresso*; Felipe Ferre's *Il Caffè*; Ralph Hattox's *Coffee and Coffeehouses, The Origins of a Social Beverage in the Medieval Near East;* and Mariarosa Schiaffino's *Le Ore del Caffè* and *Cioccolato & Cioccolatini*. Finally, the works of Michael Sivetz and William Ukers continue to be invaluable.

The notes and records of the ongoing saga of coffee and coffee culture recorded in *Café Olé* magazine, *Fresh Cup* magazine, and *Tea and Coffee Trade Journal* were constantly useful, as were the publications of the Specialty Coffee Association of America.

I am delighted to have an opportunity to thank the California College of Arts and Crafts for supporting my research in Italy, and those at Cole Group who assisted me, including my patient editor Annette Gooch; production director Steve Lux; his assistant and art editor Dotti Hydue; Dee Dee Ford, marketing coordinator; and head creative schmoozer and publisher James Connolly. I also would like to acknowledge Michael Surles, illustrator; Paul Schulz, photographer and founder of San Francisco's Caffè Soma, who somehow managed to take the cover shot before the *crema* broke up; and Emanuela Aureli, who graciously assisted me with telephone calls to Italy.

A concluding word of gratitude to those many others whose insight has enriched and enlivened my view of espresso, even though I may have lost their cards or misplaced my scribbles on the backs of product literature. The achievements of this book belong entirely to those who assisted me; only the mistakes are mine.

CHAPTER 1

SOME DEFINITIONS

Espresso Break

The Espresso Bar System

Definitions can be peculiarly detached from actual experience. At the level at which we genuinely live life, rather than simply think about it, every reader of this book will have a different definition of espresso. For some, that definition may be a long-developed acquaintance with the beverage, an accumulation of happy memories of caffès and tinkering with home machines, of frothed milk and crema. For others, "espresso" may mean a single experience with a caffè latte taken at an outdoor espresso stand during a vacation or a couple of cappuccinos drunk while on a trip to Italy. Like coffee itself, espresso is as much an experience caught up in the intimate textures of our lives as it is a beverage.

Yet even when we attempt to define espresso in more detached fashion, there still appear to be many overlapping definitions, rather than a single, all-inclusive one.

A TECHNICAL DEFINITION

A definition of espresso along technical lines is perhaps least ambiguous: Espresso is coffee brewed from beans roasted dark brown, darker than the American norm but not black, with the brewing accomplished by hot water forced through a bed of finely ground, densely compacted coffee at a pressure of approximately nine atmospheres. The resulting heavy-bodied, aromatic, bittersweet beverage is often combined with milk that has been heated and aerated by having steam run through it until the milk is hot and covered by a head of froth.

To extend the technical definition somewhat, we might say that espresso is an entire *system* of coffee production, a *system* that includes specific approaches to blending the coffee, to roasting it, and to grinding it; and that emphasizes freshness through grinding and brewing coffee a cup at a time *on demand*, rather than brewing a pot or urn at a time from pre-ground coffee and letting the result sit until it is served.

A HISTORICAL AND CULTURAL DEFINITION

Defining espresso culturally and historically is more problematic. The taste for a dark, heavy, intense coffee, sweetened and drunk out of little cups, is obviously much older than the espresso machine itself and may stretch back as far as the first coffeehouses in Cairo, Egypt, established during the early fifteenth century. On the other hand, technology (and the imagery of technology) is also obviously an important element of espresso culture. Although all coffee-making lends itself to technological tinkering, no other coffee culture has applied technology to coffee-making with quite the passion as the Italians have to espresso. The word *espresso* itself suggests custom-brewing, as in "brewed *expressly* for you," as well as direct, rapid, nonstop, as in *express* train or letter. Not only has technology been enthusiastically

A contemporary espresso cart, an increasingly familiar sight in North American shopping malls, downtown streets, and even gasoline stations.

connected to modernity and a dynamic urbanism, as often has been the case in Italy, espresso in America has become identified with various alternative cultures, from Europeanized sophisticate nostalgically evoking tradition to intellectual rebel attacking it.

ESPRESSO AS CUISINE

Espresso can also be defined as a kind of coffee *cuisine*. For example, mainstream American coffee cuisine emphasizes large, repeated servings of brisk-tasting, light-bodied coffees prepared by the filter method, usually taken without milk or sweetener. The espresso cuisine, on the other hand, emphasizes smaller servings of heavier-bodied, richer coffee, brewed on demand rather than in batches, usually drunk sweetened, and often combined with hot, frothed milk and other garnishes and flavorings.

But once beyond the espresso-and-frothed-milk component of a culinary definition, we again encounter overlap and ambiguity. In Italy a single, national espresso cuisine emphasizing simplicity and exquisitely modulated variations on coffee and milk has largely overwhelmed most regional differences in how espresso is publicly presented. In the United States, by contrast, one can identify several espresso cuisines. The major one is the Italian-American, which resembles the Italian cuisine, yet differs from it in certain subtle but conspicuous ways. Another American espresso cuisine is the wide-open, innovative version spreading out of Seattle, in which the

applied to the actual process of brewing espresso, but the imagery of technology, the idea of modernity and speed, also turns up as a major element in espresso's cultural symbolism. See the famous Victoria Arduino poster from the 1920s on page v, for example. So culturally and historically we have a paradox. On the one hand, espresso as a general taste in coffee-drinking goes back to the very beginnings of coffee as a public beverage; on the other, Italian espresso culture has refined that taste through a technology and technological mystique that flaunts its modernity.

When we turn our attention to the United States, a historical and cultural definition of espresso might emphasize still another set of associations. Rather than being

(continued on page 7)

THE ESPRESSO BAR SYSTEM

Delivery of a tiny, aromatic cup of espresso or a perfectly balanced cappuccino depends on an integrated brewing system, including machine, grinder and accessories. The various elements of a complete commercial espresso system are illustrated on the opposite page.

The machine. The machine pictured here is a simple semiautomatic pump machine. The operator grinds the coffee, dispenses it into a metal filter fixed inside a filter holder, clamps the filter and filter holder into the machine, and triggers a switch to start and stop the flow of brewing water through the coffee. For illustrated descriptions of other types of machine, including manual piston and fully automatic, see pages 17–22.

The *housing* (1) of the machine conceals a water reservoir, a pump to push the brewing water through the coffee, apparatus for heating and measuring the brewing water, and a boiler in which the water used to create steam for milk frothing is held and heated. In this style of machine the apparatus that heat water for brewing and for steam production are separate, since the ideal water temperature for brewing is somewhat lower than the temperature required to produce steam.

The *group* (from Italian *gruppo*) or *brew head* (2) is where the *filter holder* or *portafilter* (3) and metal *filter* (4) clamp and where the actual brewing takes place. The pump inside the housing delivers heated water through a perforated plate (*shower disk*, *shower head*, or *distribution*) on the underside of the group, forcing the water through the ground coffee held in the filter and filter holder.

The filter and filter holder can be designed to produce a single serving or a double serving. In the latter case the filter is sufficiently large to contain twice the amount of ground coffee as a single, and the filter holder has two outlets. The filter holder and filter indicated by (3) and (4) are intended to produce a double serving.

The *drip tray* (5) catches coffee overflow, and the *steam valve* or *knob* (6) controls the flow of steam through the *steam wand, pipe,* or *nozzle* (7), which the operator

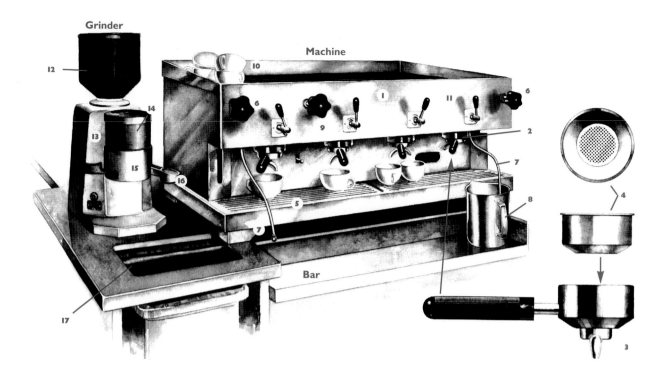

Grinder

Machine

Bar

thrusts into the *frothing* or *milk pitcher* (8) to froth and heat milk for cappuccino, caffè latte, and other drinks that combine espresso coffee with hot, frothed milk. The *hot water tap* (9) dispenses hot water for tea and similar hot drinks, and the *cup warmer* (10) stores and gently preheats cups and glasses.

The illustrated machine has a very simple *control panel* (11): a switch above each group turns the brewing water on and off. The timing of the brewing operation is up to the operator. In other machines the operator simply touches a button to select the length of the dose of brewing water (usually ranging from a single short serving to a double regular serving). A computer chip does the rest. Controls for fully automatic machines may be even more elaborate, with more options, and may include readouts that provide the operator with information concerning brewing pressure, brewing temperature, and the like. For illustrated descriptions of examples of more complex machines, see page 20.

On the other hand, manual piston machines (see page 18) provide no control panels or buttons whatsoever; the dose of brewing water is controlled by purely mechanical nonelectronic means.

The grinder. Note the conical reservoir for roasted whole beans (12); the *grinding unit* proper where the grinding burrs are concealed (13); the *cylinder* where the recently ground coffee is held (14), hopefully for only a few minutes; the *doser* (15), which measures one *dose,* or serving's worth, of ground coffee at the flick of a lever; and the *tamper, presser,* or *packer* (16), which is used to distribute and compress the coffee in the filter. Some bar systems may add a second grinder for decaffeinated beans, but if demand for decaffeinated drinks is light, the second grinder may be replaced, as it is here, by a simple container of pre-ground decaffeinated coffee kept close at hand.

The bar. In addition to supporting the machine and grinder, the bar unit also includes a *knock-out* or *dump box* (17), into which the operator disposes of spent coffee grounds by inverting the filter holder and knocking it sharply against the edge of the box. The knock-out box may sit atop the counter next to the machine, or it may be built into the structure of the bar, as it is here.

basic themes of espresso and milk have been exuberantly elaborated with flavored syrups, ice, a score of garnishes, and seemingly endless refinements involving the milk. Still another, more regional American espresso cuisine is the Cuban tradition of south Florida. Finally, one could argue that there is still a fourth American cuisine, which I would like to dub *espresso manqué*, and which is all of the misinterpretations and misunderstandings of espresso being committed in the United States today thrown together, including watery, bitter, overextracted coffee; scalded milk; meringue-like heads of froth, all presented to the background flatulence of canned whipped cream being sprayed on top of the drink to distract us from the grim reality underneath.

A DEFINITION BY PLACE

One could define espresso in terms of the places it has helped create and that helped create it: the caffès, cafés, coffeehouses, espresso bars, and espresso carts of the world. For espresso is a quintessentially public coffee. The technological sophistication of the espresso system as it began to develop between the two World Wars could have evolved only in the context of public establishments with sufficient numbers of coffee drinkers to support the expense involved in maintaining such large and complex coffee-making equipment. Thus espresso and the

espresso machine have come to constitute the spiritual and aesthetic heart of a variety of subtly different institutions, including the Italian-American caffè, the espresso bar, the American coffeehouse, and now the Seattle-style espresso cart and stand.

THE NICE VICE

I'm drawn to add still one more definition, something along contemporary sociological lines. For it appears that fancy coffees generally and espresso cuisine in particular have assumed a rather unique role in contemporary American life. It is a role that has led some commentators to characterize coffee (and caffeine) as the "nice vice" of the 1990s, the one pleasantly consciousness-altering substance that has somehow escaped the censure heaped by the right-minded public on alcohol, tobacco, and their various illegal alternatives. Certainly the current crop of college-age youth, a generation I find particularly attractive, has adopted coffee as a beverage and ritual of choice. Fifties-style coffeehouses are booming, and wherever younger people congregate, T-shirts and lapel buttons surface, half-seriously, half-ironically celebrating coffee. "Espresso Yourself" says one; "Coffee is God" proclaims another.

So is everything else, the Buddhist might reply, but coffee and espresso do seem a little special.

CHAPTER 2

The Cultural Context

Enter Technology

Breaking the 1 ½ Atmospheres Ceiling

Information-Age Espresso

Domestic Espresso

A BRIEF HISTORY

Espresso Breaks

The Caffè Giants

Two Centuries of Home Espresso Brewers

*F*rom a cultural point of view, the history of espresso extends back several centuries, to the beginnings of Mediterranean coffee-drinking tradition. If we look at espresso history from a more technical point of view, however, the horizon moves closer, either to the nineteenth century and the first coffeepots that used the pressure of trapped steam to force water through a compressed bed of ground coffee, or to the mid-twentieth century, when Achille Gaggia introduced the first commercial machines to use a spring-loaded piston to force the hot water through the coffee at pressures even greater than could be achieved with trapped steam.

THE CULTURAL CONTEXT

Italians are wont to give the impression that the development of espresso was a purely rational, inevitable process, driven by technical factors alone, aimed at producing the best possible cup of coffee. However, the various North American and European technicians who developed the automatic filter-drip system might make the same argument for the process through which they perfected their brewing method.

Cultures and individuals choose to roast, brew, and drink coffee the way they do for reasons that are largely irrational. There is no intrinsic culinary logic or technical rationale for preferring "Turkish"-style coffee over espresso, for example, or for preferring either espresso or Turkish-style coffee over American-style filter coffee. Each

of these coffee-drinking traditions represents a somewhat different cultural definition of "coffee."

A Certain Technical and Sensual Logic

It would seem, however, that once a culture has settled on a collective definition of coffee, a certain technical and sensual logic comes into play. Given the traditional North American definition of coffee, for example, we probably can say that automatic filter-drip coffee is "better" than percolator coffee, because given North American tastes the filter-drip coffee is brighter, clearer, and more aromatic than the percolator coffee, which has been perked to death, as it were. But I doubt whether a coffee drinker from either Yemen or Milan would consider either filter or percolator coffee much better than insipid hot water. Good espresso is neither bright nor clear like North American filter coffee, nor is it somewhat soupy and full of grounds like Turkish-style brew. Good espresso has its own peculiar set of criteria for goodness.

The Idea of Espresso

Thus we must begin by tracing the taste for the kind of coffee that *became* espresso, for the *idea* of espresso, before we take up the technical developments that brought that taste or idea to perfection.

When coffee first made its appearance in human culture, it was almost certainly as medicinal herb in the natural medicine chest of the peoples of the horn of Africa, in what is now Somalia and Ethiopia. For until the fifteenth century, when Arab peoples in what is now Yemen learned to take this seed of a humble little berry, roast it, grind it, and combine it with hot water, it doubtless had little appeal to the human senses beyond its effect as stimulant. And even roasted, ground, and brewed, coffee is a hard sell to the taste buds at first encounter. I know of no evidence indicating that the human organism "likes" its first taste of coffee. Like many other beverages, coffee appears to be an acquired taste.

Perhaps this is the reason that fairly early in coffee's history, sugar was added to the cup. The earliest accounts of coffee brewing in Arabia, Egypt, Syria, and Turkey seem to suggest that, although adding sugar or even milk (most likely goat's milk) to the cup was not unknown, coffee was generally drunk either straight or with the addition of perfume or spice, most often cardamom. The "Turkish" coffee we are familiar with today, in which finely powdered coffee and varying proportions of sugar are brought to a boil several times in a small pot, then dispensed into tiny cups, apparently took hold in the seventeenth century in Egypt and Turkey. This style of coffee, which eventually came to dominate the coffee cultures of the Middle East, North Africa, and Southeastern Europe, is drunk without separating the grounds from the coffee. The coffee is served very hot and covered by a head of froth produced by the repeated boiling. By the time the liquid is cool enough to drink, the powdered coffee grounds largely have settled to the bottom of the cup, leaving only a slight, pleasantly bitter suspension of grit in the drink.

Although the differences between a demitasse of Turkish-style coffee and a demitasse of espresso may be rather striking, yet so are the similarities. In both cases, a

A Middle Eastern or "Turkish" coffee set. The object in the middle is the ibrik (Turkish) or briki (Greek), in which finely powdered coffee, water, and (usually) sugar are brought to a foamy boil. The resulting strong, frothy suspension is poured from the ibrik into the little cups.

rather darkly roasted coffee is drunk out of small cups; in both cases the coffee is heavy-bodied and usually taken sweetened; in both cases a good deal of emphasis is placed on the froth that covers the coffee (in the case of espresso, the *crema*; in Turkish-style coffee, the *kaymak*, to use the Turkish term).

Cow's Milk and Strained Coffee

It is to Christian Europe's military standoff and love-hate relationship with the Ottoman Turks that we can attribute both the spread of coffee to Western Europe and the use of the term "Turkish" to describe a style of coffee now drunk over a large part of Eurasia and Africa. In fact, tradition ascribes the habit of adding milk to coffee, which figures so importantly in North America's growing love affair with espresso cuisine, to the failed siege of Vienna by the Turks in 1683. After the siege was lifted, Franz

George Kolschitzky, a Polish hero in the struggle, supposedly opened the first Viennese cafés with coffee left behind by the Turks. According to tradition, Kolschitzky first tried to serve his booty Turkish-style, grounds and all, but was forced to innovate by straining the coffee and adding milk to it in order to lure townspeople into the first of the famous Viennese cafés.

Historians have turned up earlier references to the use of milk in coffee, but in a real, cultural sense, legend is most likely correct in attributing the beginning of the practice to Kolschitzky. Others may have experimented with adding milk to coffee, but the widespread popular tradition of drinking strained coffee with cow's milk probably did begin in Vienna in the seventeenth century, and spread from there into Western Europe, while the areas of Eastern Europe and the Mediterranean that remained under Ottoman Turk control until later centuries (the

A nineteenth-century depiction of the Caffè Florian in Venice's Piazza San Marco. Founded in 1720, the Caffè Florian was one of Europe's first coffeehouses, and survives today virtually intact.

Balkans, Hungary, Greece, Egypt, present-day Turkey, Lebanon, etc.) continue until this day to drink coffee in the "Turkish" style. This clear demarcation of coffee-drinking habits, with most areas east of Vienna still taking their coffee Turkish-style with grounds, and most regions west of Vienna taking their coffee strained, often with milk, would seem to indicate that the innovation in coffee-drinking that took place in Vienna in the seventeenth century was decisive in the history of coffee habits in Western Europe.

Coffee Comes to Italy

Coffee was first imported into Europe on a commercial scale through Venice beginning in the seventeenth century; as a consequence Venice developed Europe's first coffeehouses, one of which, Caffè Florian (1720), is still extant, delighting tourists and lightening them of quantities of *lire*. Although Caffè Florian today serves the classic Italian espresso cuisine, with a "latte" or two thrown in for the North Americans, the early Venetian caffès almost certainly served coffee in the Turkish style, boiled with sugar and drunk with the grounds settled to the bottom of the cup.

It is doubtless the very powerful Austrian influence in Northern Italy in the eighteenth and nineteenth centuries that created a taste for filtered coffee and coffee mixed with milk. Austria controlled Milan, the ultimate center of espresso innovation, from 1714 to 1860, with only a brief interruption of French rule under Napoleon.

Still, it is tempting to see a lingering Turkish influence in the modern Italian obsession with *crema*, the finely textured brown froth that covers the surface of a well-brewed espresso. The culture of Turkish-style coffee puts a similar emphasis on the froth, called in Turkish *kaymak*, in Greek *kaimaki*. In both the espresso and Turkish-style coffee cuisines, to serve coffee without a proper covering of froth is a sign of culinary impotence, bad manners, or both.

Nevertheless, it would seem that the Austrian influence is most important in the genesis of espresso, for although Italians continued to enjoy coffee strong, sweetened, and in small cups, the fact that they filtered their coffee and often added hot milk to it is of the utmost importance in understanding the development of espresso cuisine.

Liberation of a Coffee Ideal

For it is on this cultural premise, i.e., a taste for coffee that is strong and heavy-bodied, yet filtered, and often combined with hot milk, that the great espresso cuisine of Northern Italy developed. It is as though the ideal of espresso was somehow present from the moment northern Italians developed a taste for strong, heavy-bodied, yet filtered coffee. The rest of the technical history of espresso can be seen as a gradual achievement of that goal, a liberating of it, as it were, from the shackles of technical limitation.

In fact, if one wanted to indulge in irresponsible historical generalization, one could say that this taste for heavy-bodied yet filtered coffee represents a typically Italian maximization of the two cultural strains—the Eastern Mediterranean (Byzantine and Arab) and the Western European—that together have made Italian culture such a continually fascinating and creative blend. The Eastern Mediterranean influence is seen in the cultural premise of small cups of heavy-bodied coffee drunk sweetened and covered with froth; the Western European in the practice of filtering the coffee and often combining it with cow's milk, and in the almost obsessive tendency to apply technological innovation to the brewing process.

ENTER TECHNOLOGY

It is at this point, during the nineteenth century, that the cultural history of espresso also becomes a history of espresso technology. Though tinkering and gadget making have been part of coffee culture almost from its very inception, the scale and thoroughness with which espresso cuisine utilizes technology remains unprecedented and is undoubtedly one of the principal sources of its fascination for the rest of the world.

By the time of the industrial revolution during the late eighteenth and early nineteenth century, coffee drinking was a well-established habit, and it was inevitable that the ritual of coffee brewing would provoke the interest of the tinkerers and inventors of the period.

Improving the Filter Pot

The starting point for many of these coffee-making innovations was the by now familiar drip or filter pot, in which the simple pull of gravity causes hot water to trickle down through a bed of coffee loosely laid over a metal or ceramic filter. There are several drawbacks to the filter-drip method. One is the slowness of the process. If the coffee is ground too finely, the brewing process may even stop altogether, and the impatient coffee lover is forced to knock the pot around or stir the grounds in an effort to speed things up. Not only is the drip method slow, but it is also relatively costly and inefficient, since the rather coarse grind demanded by the method means a less thorough extraction than could be achieved with a finer grind.

For these reasons, efforts to apply the technologies of the early industrial revolution to coffee making often involve expediting the drip process by either pulling the hot water through the problematic bed of ground coffee (via a partial vacuum) or by pushing it through by various expedients, including compressed air, hand-operated plungers, and the pressure of trapped steam.

Pulling and Pushing

By the 1840s the pulling approach was in use in several versions of what is now known as the vacuum brewer. The version by Robert Napier, the Scots inventor of the steam engine, is best known. Napier's original device looks more like a steam engine than a coffee maker, but as it has evolved today, the vacuum brewer consists of two glass globes that fit tightly together, one above the other, with a cloth or metal filter between. The ground coffee is placed in the upper globe, and water is brought to boil in the lower. The two globes are fitted together and the heat is lowered. Pressure develops as water

vapor expands in the lower globe, forcing the water into the upper globe, where it mixes with the ground coffee. After one to three minutes, the pot is removed from the heat, and the partial vacuum formed in the lower globe pulls the brewed coffee back down through the filter, accelerating the drip process and permitting use of a finer grind of coffee, which in turn attains a more thorough extraction than can be achieved by the simple drip method.

Other coffee-maker tinkerers pursued the opposite approach. Rather than making use of a partial vacuum to pull the hot water through the bed of coffee, their devices applied pressure to the hot water to push it through. Many of these early nineteenth-century designs anticipate solutions applied later in espresso technology. In some, for example, a hand-operated piston forces water through the bed of coffee. In others, compressed air manually pumped into the hot water chamber provides the brewing pressure.

The method that eventually prevailed in the early espresso technology, however, was one that utilized the trapped pressure of steam. Water brought to a boil inside a sealed chamber created steam; the confined steam then forced the water through the bed of coffee. A glance at the cutaway illustration on page 108 of a simple Italian Moka-style coffee pot of today gives a general idea of how these early small steam-pressure devices worked. The first European patents for small home devices using the steam-pressure principle were filed between 1818 and 1824. Various ingenious refinements to the steam pressure principle were proposed, forgotten, and proposed all over again throughout the nineteenth century, but all remained either commercially unexploited or applied only to small-scale home brewers. It was not until the early years of the twentieth century that the steam pressure principle was finally successfully applied to a large commercial machine, and the technology and culture of caffè espresso was born.

The Precursors of the Espresso Machine

The first large caffè machine to utilize a variation on the steam pressure principle is credited to Edward Loysel de Santais, who at the Paris Exposition in 1855 demonstrated a machine that used the pressure of trapped steam not to directly force the brewing water through the coffee, but rather to raise the water to a considerable height above the coffee, from whence it descended through an elaborate system of tubes to the coffee bed. The weight of the hot water, not the trapped steam, applied the brewing pressure. Santais's complex machine brewed "two thousand cups of coffee in an hour," according to one awestruck contemporary observer. It apparently brewed coffee a potful at a time, however, just as many French cafés today still brew their espresso. Despite its impressive technology, Santais's device apparently was too complex and difficult to operate to have any lasting influence on public coffee-making.

Various Northern Italians persisted in attempting to improve on machines like Santais's device and the smaller steam pressure brewers, however. Why the Northern Italians continued in this effort, when it was largely dropped elsewhere in favor of other coffee-brewing methods, is a matter for speculation. It may be that the Italians, latecomers to the imperialist game and consequently without the coffee-growing colonies possessed by France and England, were forced to compensate for the high cost and relatively poor quality of their coffee imports with superior brewing technology. Or it may be that for cultural reasons, perhaps related to the strong Eastern Mediterranean influence, Italians simply craved a fuller-bodied cup than North Americans and other Europeans and continued to evolve technology to achieve that end.

The Bezzera Breakthrough

The next important date in the technical development of espresso is 1901, when the Milanese Luigi Bezzera patented a steam-pressure restaurant machine that distributed the coffee through one or more "water and steam groups" *directly into the cup.* In many respects the Bezzera machine established the basic configuration that espresso machines would maintain until the development of today's fully automatic machines. A glance at the illustrations on page 17 reveals the familiar filter holder, the "group" into which the filter holder and filter clamp, the steam valve and wand, etc. The Bezzera design also established the emphasis on freshness and drama characteristic of the espresso system: The coffee is custom-brewed by the cup for customers before their eyes. Again, this feature of espresso culture intriguingly suggests another aspect of the Turkish-style coffee culture: In traditional Middle Eastern coffeehouses the coffee is always brewed by the cup, on demand. At any rate, the concept of freshly ground coffee brewed on demand has remained a central element of the espresso system ever since Bezzera's innovation.

The Bezzera patent was acquired in 1903 by Desiderio Pavoni, who began manufacturing machines based on the Bezzera design in 1905. Pier Teresio Arduino started producing similar machines soon afterwards, and other manufacturers followed. By the 1920s these familiar, towering, ornament-topped machines dominated the Italian caffè scene.

Espresso-Powered Imagery

This was the period too during which the imagery of espresso as a symbol of urban speed and energy first emerged. The famous Victoria Arduino poster of 1922 reproduced on page v seems to sum up every nuance of these associations: the romantic power of steam driving both locomotive and espresso (espresso machines of the period often literally resemble sleek locomotives set on end), while the sophisticated urbanite, espresso-powered, as it were, rockets his way on a *tazzina* of coffee through the urban machine without a wasted second. Occasionally the work of the Italian Futurist movement betrays in the midst of its celebration of urban speed and potency a similar association with coffee. The 1910 painting by Umberto Boccioni, "Riot in the Galleria," reproduced on page 23, represents a sort of well-dressed brawl in front of a caffè. It explodes not only with the almost hysterical energy of the city, but with the powerful excitement of coffee (and presumably of the new culture of espresso) as well. Note how light shoots from the caffè like spikes of some frenzied indoor mental sun.

BREAKING THE 1½ ATMOSPHERES CEILING

Throughout the period between the wars, however, there were signs that Italian coffee innovators were not content with the 1½ atmospheres of pressure exerted on the brewing water by trapped steam alone. The pressure could be increased to some degree by increasing the heat and thus the steam pressure, but this intensified heat often cooked or baked the ground coffee during the brewing process. It was also generally known that boiling was not the optimum temperature for water used in brewing coffee and that a smoother extraction of the flavor oils could be obtained by a water temperature short of boiling. Both of these concerns argued for a method of applying pressure to the brewing water other than that supplied by trapped steam.

The most commercially successful of these between-the-wars attempts to increase brewing pressure involved making use of the simple power of water run from the tap. Called "electro-instantaneous" machines, these devices used electric elements to rapidly heat tap water to brewing temperature in miniature boilers, one boiler to each brewing group. Each boiler was separately connected to the tap. When the operator tripped a lever above a group, the backed-up pressure from the tap forced the hot water in the little boiler out through the ground coffee. Depending on the strength of the local water pressure, such machines could exert considerably

(continued on page 24)

THE CAFFÈ GIANTS

In Italy the great espresso machines of the past evoke the same rush of admiration and nostalgia that certain old automobiles and jukeboxes do in the United States. The six machines that follow represent either key developments or general trends in the history of the caffè espresso machine.

1920s and 1930s

La Pavoni. A machine typical of those manufactured in the 1920s by Pavoni, Victoria Arduino, and many other firms. Machines like this one essentially created espresso culture and carried it across Europe and the Americas. Steam pressure is generated in the giant gas-fired boiler (see the cross-section illustration on page 21), which forces hot water through the coffee, held in a filter holder almost identical to those still used in machines today. A glance at the detail photograph of the brewing group reveals that these machines defined the general structure of the external apparatus of the espresso machine until the recent advent of the fully automatic machine. Note, for example, the familiar shape of the group, the filter holder, and the steam wand. Only the lever operating the coffee valve, reminiscent of a steam engine throttle, differs from the various levers and buttons that control coffee output in later machines.

Although these machines forced water through the coffee at a paltry 1½ atmospheres, compared to the 9 or more atmospheres considered ideal today, they introduced several innovations that carried the day for espresso: a richer coffee, brewed under pressure; a fresher coffee, custom-brewed by the cup; and milk heated by having steam run

La Pavoni Espresso Machine

Early Gaggia Spring-Piston Machine

through it, eliminating the flat taste acquired by milk heated in the conventional manner and adding the possibility of an attractive head of froth. The beauty and drama of these machines, rising toward the ceiling like gleaming towers, surrounded by wisps of steam and the elegant movements of the barista, undoubtedly further contributed to their success.

1940s and 1950s

Early Gaggia Spring-Piston Machine. Soon after World War II, the Milanese Achille Gaggia produced the first commercially successful machine to press hot water through the bed of finely granulated coffee at six to nine times the pressure generated by trapped steam alone. Gaggia's machine used a piston powered by a spring. The spring was compressed by a lever; the barista pulled down the lever, and as the spring-driven piston pressed the water through the coffee the lever returned majestically to its upright position. See the cross-section illustration on page 21.

The slogan on the machine reads "Crema Caffè/Naturale" ("Natural Coffee Cream"). This slogan refers not to the addition of actual cream to the coffee but rather to the dense golden froth, or *crema*, "naturally" covering the surface of the espresso, a sign of richness and a symptom of the greater brewing pressure achieved by the new Gaggia design.

1950s and early 1960s

Cimbali Hydraulic Machine. In 1956 the Cimbali company introduced the world's first hydraulically powered piston espresso machine. The piston was powered by the simple force of tap water; see the illustration on page 22. The earliest hydraulic machines, like the one on the left, were complex and extroverted in their exterior design, and required the operator to closely control the various phases of the brewing cycle. Later versions were almost completely automatic, requiring only the pressing of a switch to initiate the brewing operation.

Cimbali Hydraulic Machine

1960s and 1970s

The FAEMA E61. The momentous decade of the 1960s was heralded in the espresso world by the introduction of the FAEMA E61, a machine lavish with innovation. The water was heated on demand, rather than held hot in a large tank or boiler; a pump rather than a spring-driven piston supplied the brewing pressure; a decalcification system prevented the pump and heating mechanism from becoming fouled by hard water deposits; and hot water from the boiler circulating through the group, maintained an even operating temperature in its metal components. Despite the advanced, automated nature of the machine's operation, the group, pictured in the inset photograph, retained some of the extroverted, romantic look of the brewing apparatus on earlier machines. Brewing was controlled by the little lever to the right of the filter holder.

FAEMA E61 Machine

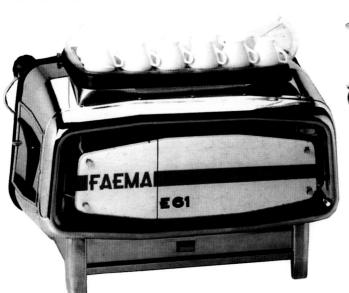

1980s and 1990s

Semiautomatic and Automatic Machines. The machine on the top left is typical of many evolved in the 1980s by numerous manufacturers. The operator still must dose and tamp the coffee, but the brewing process itself is controlled by microchip and button. Note the line of six buttons above each group. In the case of this machine the operator can, from left to right, select a single short serving (the button displays a ⅓-filled cup), a double short serving, a single regular serving, two regular servings; initiate a continuous flow of water through the coffee; or stop the operation entirely.

Typical Semiautomatic Machine:
Nuova Simonelli MAC Digit

Other machines may present considerably more complex control panels and options. The USA-made Acorto 990, on the bottom left, is perhaps a trendsetter: a fully automatic machine designed with the new Seattle or North American cuisine in mind. Several European manufacturers also produce fully automatic machines, but most of the European automatics still leave the milk frothing to the barista. The Acorto will brew the coffee, froth the milk, and assemble up to 22 different espresso drinks, ranging from short espresso to mammoth caffè lattes, in either regular or decaffeinated versions. Note the twin bean silos, one for regular and one for decaffeinated beans. The machine also incorporates refrigeration for the milk component.

Acorto 990 Machine

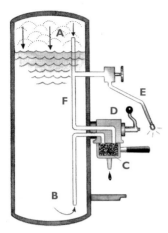

Steam Pressure Machine

Ninety Years of Espresso Technology

On the top left is a cross-section of a typical steam pressure machine of the kind popularized by Pavoni and Victoria Arduino in the early part of the twentieth century and described on page 17. Steam trapped in the gas-fired central boiler (A) presses downward on the hot brewing water, forcing it up a pipe (B) and through the compressed bed of coffee (C) when the operator opens a valve (D). The upper part of the boiler is tapped to provide steam for frothed milk drinks through the familiar steam wand (E). After brewing, steam from the upper part of the boiler is directed via another pipe (F) through the spent coffee grounds so as to dry them into a tidy cake that pops out of the filter without clumsy digging or rinsing. This step was not incorporated in later machine designs because the stronger brewing pressure generated by the more advanced machines tended to compress and dry the spent grounds automatically.

The famous Gaggia manual spring-piston machine (page 18) was introduced soon after World War II. The drawing on the bottom left shows a cross-section of such a machine. When the operator depresses the lever (A), a spring (B) is compressed above the piston (C), drawing hot water into the cylinder (D) below the piston. The spring then forces the piston back down, pressing the hot water through the bed of ground coffee. The hot water is drawn from a tank similar to the boiler in the Pavoni steam pressure machine, although in most manual piston machines the boiler is laid on its side inside a streamlined housing. As with the Pavoni and all later designs, the boiler also provides steam for milk frothing.

The first hydraulic espresso machine was introduced by the Cimbali company in 1956. Like the Gaggia-style spring-piston machines, the hydraulic machines use a piston to force the hot water through the coffee bed. However, in the Cimbali and later hydraulic designs the piston is powered by tap water, and the long lever replaced by a dial or switch. See the illustration on page 22, top, a cross-section detail of a typical hydraulic brewing group. Tap water introduced alternately above and below the large piston forces it up and down. The large piston drags the smaller piston below with it, and the smaller piston forces the hot water through the coffee.

When the operator activates the switch beginning the brew cycle, the valve at (E) allows *tap* water (not hot water from the tank) to enter the larger cylinder at (A),

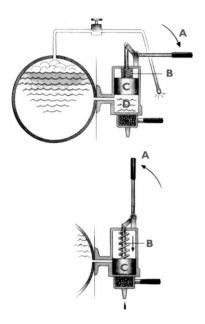

Manual Spring-Piston Machine

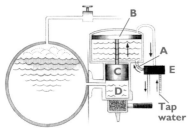

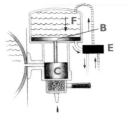

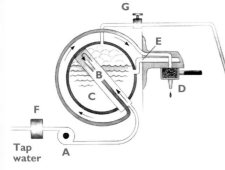

Hydraulic Espresso Machine

Electric Pump Espresso Machine

forcing the larger piston (B) upwards. The larger piston lifts the smaller piston (C), allowing hot water from the tank to enter the small cylinder at (D). When the appropriate volume of brewing water has flowed into the small cyclinder, a mechanical trigger is tripped, directing the valve at (E) to route tap water into the larger cylinder above the piston at (F). This new influx of water forces the large piston down, pushing the tap water below the piston out, and forcing the hot water in the smaller cylinder down through the coffee.

However, the future, or at least a large part of it, belonged to the electric pump design introduced in 1960 by the FAEMA company. The basic configuration of the FAEMA E61 is still used in the majority of caffè espresso machines manufactured in the world today. A cross-section typical of such machines is represented on the bottom left. Here an electric rotary pump (A) rather than a piston provides the brewing pressure. The pump forces cold water into a heat exchanger (B), a largish tube that is surrounded by the hot water of the familiar boiler (C). The cold water inside the exchanger is heated by the surrounding hot water, but is untouched by it, and is forced by continued pressure from the pump into the brewing group (D) and through the coffee. Steam for frothing continues to be supplied by the boiler. A line from the boiler (E) also maintains uniform heat in the brewing group with a convection current of hot water, and a water softening unit (F) keeps the pump and lines from becoming fouled with mineral deposits. Steam for milk frothing is supplied in the usual way by tapping the top of the boiler (G).

In pump machines manufactured today electronic instrumentation often controls the volume and temperature of the brewing water. Some machines may substitute a second boiler in place of the heat-exchanger so as to maintain greater control over brewing temperature. Fully automatic machines grind, load, and tamp the coffee for brewing. Nevertheless, all of these sophisticated machines are built around the fundamental electric pump technology introduced in 1960 by the FAEMA E61.

In this painting by Umberto Boccioni ("Riot in the Galleria," 1910) dazzling light radiates from a caffè, illuminating a frenzied city scene of the kind favored by the Italian Futurists. It is tempting to see a connection between the new culture of espresso and the nervous urban energy celebrated by the Futurists in paintings like this one.

more than the 1½ atmospheres generated by steam pressure machines.

These devices maintained the same vertical profile as the steam pressure machines but were smaller and reflected the art deco and art moderne design trends of the late 1920s and 1930s, with straight lines and dramatic geometries replacing the art nouveau curves of the earlier steam pressure machines.

Other efforts to beat the 1½ atmospheres ceiling involved a revival of the use of compressed air. A charming little home machine in the possession of Milanese collector Ambrogio Fumagalli, for example, uses an air pump to apply pressure to the brewing water, and dates from between the wars (see page 31). And in 1938, Francesco Illy built the "Illetta," a large, sophisticated commercial machine making use of compressed air.

In the same year, however, two coffee tinkerers in Milan were pursuing a direction that would have considerably more impact on espresso history. The details of their story are not entirely clear, but the ultimate outcome was a new approach to espresso brewing that would completely transform the drink and its technology.

Spring-Powered Espresso

In the years before World War II a Signore Cremonesi patented a device that forced water through the coffee by means of a screw-like piston. When a horizontal lever was turned, it forced a piston downward in a screwing motion, pushing the brewing water, which had been injected between the piston and the filter, down through the coffee. Meanwhile Achille Gaggia, a Milanese caffè

owner, was experimenting with a similar device at about the same time. The Gaggia device could be bolted onto other manufacturers' machines, in effect replacing the old steam-pressure brewing group with the new screw-down version.

World War II interrupted Cremonesi's and Gaggia's experiments, and during that time Cremonesi died, leaving the rights to his patent to his widow, Rosetta Scorza. It is not clear whether Scorza shared her dead husband's ideas with Gaggia, or whether Gaggia simply proceeded on his own, but at any rate by 1947 Gaggia had taken the original idea of the piston suggested by both inventors and transformed it into his revolutionary "lever group." The piston was now powered by a powerful spring rather than laborious screw. The operator pulled down a longish lever, which simultaneously compressed the spring and drew hot water into the chamber between the piston and the coffee. As the spring above the piston expanded, it forced the piston down, pushed the hot water through the coffee, and allowed the lever to return majestically to its original erect position. See page 21 for a cross-section of a typical spring-piston mechanism.

In 1948 Gaggia brought out the first complete machines to incorporate his new device. They were an almost instant success and apparently were responsible for the creation of the mystique of the crema in Italian coffee culture. Note the art moderne lines and the logo on the 1948 Gaggia machine pictured on page 18, proclaiming: "Crema Caffè/Naturale" ("Natural Coffee Cream"). What constituted "unnatural" coffee cream I have no idea. Perhaps the question could be asked only by a foreigner; the emphasis is clearly on crema as a natural part of the brewing process, an evidence of richness. Historical anecdote suggests that Gaggia's crema slogan was a way of turning a liability into an asset. According to these stories, when people asked what that peculiar scum was floating on their coffee, Gaggia and his associates called it "coffee cream," suggesting that his new method produced coffee so rich that, in effect, the coffee produced its very own cream. Whatever the truth of that story, ever since Gaggia's time "crema" has become the mark of properly brewed espresso.

The success of the Gaggia design is understandable. It finally achieved the implicit goal toward which espresso cuisine had been aspiring—the easy richness, smoothness, and full body of classic espresso. It achieved this goal by pushing the brewing water through an even more tightly packed bed of coffee than before, at a much greater pressure than ever before, assuring the rapid, complete extraction of the flavor oils characteristic of the mature espresso method.

A Performance Opportunity

What is less commonly recognized is that the Gaggia-style machines also produced one of coffee's greatest performance opportunities. The muscular pull on the lever and its slow return to an upright position became the signature performance of the *barista* of the streamlined new espresso bars that were replacing the more spacious (and doubtless more gracious) caffès and neighborhood bars of less hurried pre-World War II days. The boilers were

smaller in the new machines and were laid on their sides inside sleek housings, further reinforcing the updated image of speed, power, and modernity projected by the new brewing technology.

One could argue that all developments since Gaggia's breakthrough are mere refinements. Certainly one can make as good an espresso with a piston-style machine as with any later machine, and owing to their simplicity, ease of maintenance, and the control they permit the skilled operator, many piston machines continue to be used. Some of the better caffès in the United States still prefer the piston machines.

Automation and Speed

Nevertheless, since the day of its introduction the effort to improve the Gaggia design has never ceased. Most effort had gone into automating the process and speeding it up. The next substantial breakthrough was the introduction in 1956 of the hydraulic machine of the Cimbali company. The new Cimbali design took the idea of tap water pressure from the "electro-instantaneous" machines of the 1920s and 30s, and combined it with Gaggia's piston. The Cimbali machine actually used two pistons in two separate cylinders. The larger, upper piston was manipulated up and down by running tap water under it or above it. This larger piston was connected to a smaller piston in a second cylinder. The second, smaller piston pushed the hot water through the coffee as the larger piston was raised and lowered by the flow of tap water. See page 22, top for a cross-section drawing. Although the hydraulic design appears complicated when represented on paper, it is in fact a simple, durable technology still in use today.

The main advances embodied by the hydraulic design are convenience (the operator has only to flip a switch rather than pull on a long handle) and precise control over the volume of brewing water allowed to flow through the coffee. When the hot water inside the smaller brewing cylinder reaches a predetermined volume selected by the operator (enough for a short serving, for example, or a regular serving) a notch in the slowly moving double-piston mechanism triggers a valve that reverses the flow of tap water from below the larger piston to above, thus reversing the direction of the larger piston, terminating the filling process in the smaller cylinder, and beginning the brewing with an exactly measured volume of water.

The FAEMA E61

Despite its technological and commercial success, the Cimbali design was soon upstaged by the introduction in 1960 of the famous E61 machine of Ernesto Valente's FAEMA company, the first espresso device to use an electric pump to force the hot water through the coffee. The E61 also incorporated several other features that were not original to the Valente machine but in their collective impact were revolutionary.

The most important was a method of heating brewing water in small batches by means of a device called a *heat-exchanger*. Recall that the Gaggia-style machines heated the water used for both brewing and steam production in a large tank or boiler at the heart of the machine, a disad-

vantage because the water sometimes became saline or stale when held in the tank for long periods. The heat-exchanger is a tube that carries fresh water through the tank of already hot, "old" water. As the electric pump pushes fresh water through this tube, it is heated by the surrounding water of the tank yet is protected by the tube from contamination. Thus water is delivered hot but fresh to the brewing group. Meanwhile, the hot water in the tank is used only for producing steam for milk-frothing.

Another of the technical elements that made the Valente design successful was the use of a decalcification process to soften the water before it entered the pump and heating apparatus, thus preventing the mechanism from being fouled by lime deposits. Finally, the Valente design circulated hot water from the tank through concealed cavities in the brewing group, thus assuring that the group would maintain an even temperature for every cup brewed, whether it be one an hour or a hundred in a row. The cross-section illustration on page 22, bottom, indicates the main interior components of the Valente design and its many successors down to the present.

Externally, the Valente FAEMA design replaced the long lever of the Gaggia design with a much smaller lever. The operator, rather than pulling on a long handle, simply activates the pump by tripping the lever, and after a suitable amount of coffee has been pressed into the cup, trips the lever a second time to end the brewing operation. For an illustration of the external features of the E61, see page 19.

Like both the Gaggia manual piston and Cimbali hydraulic designs, the FAEMA machine has been an enduring classic. Some of the original machines are still operating, and new machines using virtually the same design continue to be manufactured and sold, though by firms other than FAEMA.

INFORMATION-AGE ESPRESSO

The principal developments since the E61 have been in the direction of automation, and as industrial age modulated to information age, the computer and its potential for controlling complex, repeated operations entered the picture. The most prevalent style of machine in Italy and the United States today is usually described as a semi-automatic machine, which simply means it is a refined, push-button version of the FAEMA E61. A pump still pushes the instantly heated hot water through the coffee, though the pumping and heating operation is usually activated by a button rather than a lever. Many semi-automatic machines incorporate a computer chip and control panel, which regulate the flow of water through the coffee to produce anywhere from a single *corto,* or "short," espresso to a double *lungo,* or "long," espresso. Thus the operator is relieved by the computer of the need to cut off the flow of water through the coffee at the correct moment. For an illustrated description of a typical semiautomatic machine see page 20, top.

In the semiautomatic machine, however, the operator still loads the filter with coffee, disposes of the grounds, froths the milk, and assembles the final drink. Beginning in the 1980s, fully automatic machines have appeared, which grind, dose, and tamp the ground coffee; brew it according to the directions punched into the machine by the operator; and dispose of the grounds. With the popularity of decaffeinated coffee, particularly in Switzerland, Germany, and North America, many of the larger automatic machines incorporate two separate grinders and produce either decaffeinated or regular espresso, in any quantity, at the touch of a button. However, most of these fully automatic machines do not heat and froth the milk and assemble the final drink.

Machines That Do It All

Inevitably, machines have been developed that do it all, including frothing milk and assembling the drinks. Some are modest box-shaped devices that sit atop counters in European offices, and others are muscular coin-operated devices that lurk dutifully in airports and waiting rooms. Although these European vending and office machines do brew genuine espresso, their milk-frothing function tends to be compromised by various technical expedients. The current crop of European vending machines, for example, uses powdered rather than fresh milk.

This is not true of the made-in-USA Acorto 990, which is designed to be used in caffès and restaurants, and is the first fully automatic machine to take into account the North American taste for mammoth caffè lattes and other oversized frothed-milk-and-espresso drinks. The Acorto 990 (for an illustrated description, see page 20) uses fresh, cold milk and brews the espresso, froths the milk, and assembles the drink in authentic fashion. Kept in proper running order, the Acorto 990 produces espresso cuisine virtually indistinguishable from the production of a good barista working a semi-automatic machine in classic fashion.

However, so far most Italian and North American caffès, bars, and restaurants have stuck with the simpler manual and semiautomatic devices, at most trusting the machine to measure the water and time the brewing but leaving the loading, tamping, frothing, and assembling procedures to the operator. Italian bar operators argue that fully automatic machines cannot be trusted to administer the process with the same precision as a well-trained operator, and many also prefer to avoid the higher maintenance costs attributed to fully automatic machines. Finally, one can't underestimate the psychological importance of ritual in both Italy and North America. In both cultures, espresso means an experience as well as a beverage, and in Italy, in particular, that experience involves a skillful barista who performs the ritual of espresso with panache, and who can produce customized espresso, with each demitasse perfectly tuned to the individual customer's preferences.

Invisible, Unseen Power

The appearance of the fully automatic machines tends to reflect the reticence and gestural understatement of the information age. Rather than flaunting theatrical ornaments atop an elegant metal tower like the 1920s Bezzera/Pavoni machines, or promoting a macho pull on a long phallic handle like the 1950s Gaggia design, the machines of the 1990s present a sleek, understated cabinet and involve minimal theatrics from the operator. The vision of modernity they seem to aspire to is one of the invisible, unseen power of the computer, rather than the extraverted power of industry suggested by the earlier designs.

Of course we continue to experience the contradictions of the high-tech, high-touch paradox pointed out by Alvin Toffler in his 1970 book *Future Shock*. At the same historical moment that the espresso machines of the present express the understated, reticent power of the computer, other perfectly ordinary machines come tarted up with copper siding and various irrelevant pipes and gewgaws meant to suggest (to impressionable diners) the *belle epoque*, while still others are honest replicas of the famous machines of the recent past, like the FAEMA E61 noted earlier. Thus at the same moment that we reach toward ever greater automation and efficiency, we simultaneously clutch nostalgically at the forms and rituals of the past.

DOMESTIC ESPRESSO

From the introduction of the Bezzera/Pavoni machines at the turn of the century to the present, espresso cuisine largely has been a public phenomenon. Small home devices have usually mimicked the larger machines.

The exception may be the small, steam-pressure coffee makers of modest ambition the Italians simply call *caffettiere*, or coffeepots. From the mid-nineteenth century until the present the design of these devices has changed very little. A look at the historical examples on page 30 and the contemporary examples on pages

108–109 together gives some idea of the range and persistence of these little devices.

All work on the simple principle of the earliest caffè machines: Water is set to boiling by stove, alcohol lamp, or electric element; when steam pressure builds sufficiently inside the water chamber, it forces the water through the coffee. There is no steam valve for frothing milk; seldom is there even a means to cut off the flow of coffee. To avoid running too much water through the coffee and ruining it through overextraction, one must resort to expedients; carefully limiting the amount of water put in the reservoir, for example.

Bringing the Bar Home

But parallel to the uneventful history of these eternal little devices has been a steady development of more complex (and more expensive) machines that, as one Italian advertisement puts it, "bring the bar home." And since the machines at the bar have changed over the years, so have the home machines that imitate them.

Examples of these machines are described and illustrated on pages 30–33. Note that most of the developments in the full-sized caffè machines are mirrored here, from the little Gaggia device with a spring-loaded piston to the latest Saeco automatic. The range of aesthetic of the large machines is mirrored as well, from the extraverted steam-engine look of the Pavoni Europiccola to the no-nonsense reticence of the Saeco Super Automatica Twin.

For those considering purchasing a home machine, I give some advice on pages 106–107. Detailed suggestions on using these devices is provided in Chapter 9.

Two Centuries of Home Espresso Brewers

Italian Steam-Pressure Brewer

Steam-Pressure Brewer with Separate Coffee Chamber

Early Steam-Pressure Brewers

Italian Steam-Pressure Brewer. On the left is a design typical of many small tabletop brewing devices manufactured in northern Italy throughout the late nineteenth and early twentieth centuries. An alcohol lamp heated water in a sealed reservoir at the lower part of the device; the pressure of steam trapped in the reservoir gradually forced the water up a tube and through a bed of coffee. The brewed coffee exited from the top of the pot via the curved tube into a cup or container.

Steam-Pressure Brewer with Separate Coffee Chamber. In the later nineteenth century steam-pressure designs appeared that separated the filter containing the coffee from the water-steam reservoir, in order to avoid baking or burning the ground coffee. Most of these devices presented a profile similar to this early twentieth-century design from the collection of Ambrogio Fumagalli, Milan. The water-steam reservoir is at the right; the trapped steam pressure in the reservoir forced the water up and along the horizontal tube at the top of the device, then down through the coffee held in the filter chamber on the left.

This example, like many similar designs, incorporates an additional useful feature: a valve controlling the flow of hot water from the reservoir to the filter holding the coffee, which permitted the user to stop the brewing process at will. In the illustration, the control valve appears as a small lever at the top of the reservoir. Curiously, such means to control the output of coffee, so crucial to making flavorful espresso, is omitted in most contemporary Italian stovetop and tabletop brewers, despite its successful incorporation in relatively early examples like this one.

Compressed Air Pressure Brewer

Gaggia Spring-Loaded Piston Brewer

Pavoni Europiccola Brewer

Efforts to Achieve Greater Brewing Pressure

Compressed Air Pressure Brewer. In this device from the 1920s, the pressure of compressed air forced the brewing water through the ground coffee. Hot water was placed in the elevated central reservoir. The water was then forced through the ground coffee by means of air pumped into the top of the reservoir by the small hand pump protruding from the base on the left. A concealed tube conducted the air to the top of the reservoir, and the coffee was held near the bottom of the reservoir in a metal filter.

Gaggia Spring-Loaded Piston Brewer. Doubtless an effort by Gaggia to extend the popularity of its revolutionary new lever-operated commercial machines (see page 18) to the home market, this machine from the 1950s used a spring-loaded piston to force hot water through the tightly packed coffee, producing a near caffè-quality espresso. When the handles on either side of the device were clamped down, a spring was compressed inside the top of the central tower. The spring then forced a piston down through a reservoir filled with electrically heated water, pressing the water through the coffee, which was held in a commercial-style filter and filter holder at the bottom of the device. Also from the collection of Ambrogio Fumagalli.

Pavoni Europiccola. A charming device still being manufactured, the Europiccola combines the *belle epoque* look of the early Pavoni bar machines with a manually operated lever reminiscent of the Gaggia machines of the 1950s. The lever does not compress a spring, however, as in the Gaggia-style machines, but directly acts on the piston. In other words, the operator simply leans on the lever and presses the water through the coffee. The Europiccola and other larger, somewhat more sophisticated machines like it make excellent espresso when used knowledgeably.

Steam Pressure Brewers 1950s to the Present

"Atomic" Steam-Pressure Brewer. The name "Atomic" and the shape, reminiscent of a cross between a mushroom cloud and an overstuffed sofa, both seem to mark this device (see page 32, top) as a product of the 1950s, although similar designs had been produced earlier in the century by the same manufacturer. A stovetop machine, the Atomic used the pressure of trapped steam and a commercial-style filter and filter

"Atomic" Steam-Pressure Brewer

Braun Espresso Master

holder. The addition of a steam valve and wand for making drinks with frothed milk is unusual; most small European home espresso brewers did not, and still do not, incorporate this feature, since most Italians prefer their espresso without milk.

The addition of the steam valve made this device a strong seller in the United States and Australia in the 1960s, when espresso drinks with milk were first becoming popular in both countries. My first two home espresso brewers were Atomics, and I still feel a pang of nostalgia when I see one. The manufacturer of the Atomic is now out of business. It was a rather cranky design that required an attentive operator and some crafty improvisation to produce decent espresso; the small electric countertop devices popular today (see below) are easier to use.

The illustrated example comes from the collection of the Thomas Cara family, San Francisco. Thomas Cara, a pioneering West Coast importer and distributor of espresso apparatus, customized many of the Atomic brewers he sold by adding the little steam pressure gauge seen here protruding from the top of the machine.

Contemporary Steam-Pressure Brewer. Little electric countertop machines like this one from Braun and similar models from Krups and other European manufacturers are changing the way North Americans make their coffee. Used carefully, a device like this one, which retails for under $100, can make decent espresso drinks with frothed milk and weak but passable straight espresso. It uses the pressure of trapped steam to force the water through the coffee, just like the "Atomic" machine above and the earlier devices illustrated on page 30, but it uses an electric element to heat the water, keeps the ground coffee from baking by separating it from the body of the machine, and incorporates a steam wand for frothing milk and a valve for stopping the flow of coffee at the optimum moment to avoid overextraction. Machines like this one are a good place to start for caffè latte lovers who want to do it at home.

Like many of these small machines, the Braun Espresso Master incorporates a gadget on the end of the steam wand designed to help the neophyte successfully froth milk. See pages 135–136 for a practical discussion of these devices. In the broad historical picture, such gadgets are one more indication that espresso has gone American and that in the United States and Canada the milk-frothing operation has become as important as the coffee-making function in selling the machine.

Home Pump Machines of the 1980s and 1990s

*Baby Gaggia Home
Espresso Machine*

Baby Gaggia. This Gaggia machine from about 1980 typifies the first wave of small home pump machines to reach the North American market. It was enormously successful, particularly in Italy, where for some years few urban newlyweds found themselves without a Baby Gaggia after the presents had been opened. Sturdy and authoritative with its clean lines and cast-metal case, it attempted to bring into the home the capabilities of the semiautomatic pump machines that had come to dominate the caffè scene in the 1970s and 1980s.

Today's home pump machines tend to be smaller, lighter in weight, and cheaper (the Baby Gaggia is still manufactured, but the cast-metal case is now plastic), but they work in the same way. Water is held in a removable, refillable reservoir and flows as needed into a small boiler, where it is heated to brewing temperature and forced by means of a vibrating electric pump through the ground coffee held in a caffè-style filter and filter holder. Steam for milk frothing is produced by the same boiler, after a transitional procedure in which the temperature in the boiler is raised sufficiently to produce a sturdy flow of steam. All operations except modulating the steam flow for frothing are controlled by buttons. See page 112 for a cross-section of a typical home pump machine.

Saeco Super Automatica Twin. The Saeco Super Automatica Twin and its somewhat smaller relative, the Super Automatica, were the first fully automatic home machines to be marketed in the United States. Both operate much like the semiautomatic machines described above, but they also grind the coffee, load it, tamp it, and, after the brewing operation is completed, empty the grounds, all at the touch of various buttons. One still needs to froth the milk, however.

Saeco Super Automatica Twin

THE CAFFÈ CUISINES

Espresso Breaks

Espresso and "El Gusto Latino"
Espresso Machismo

Espresso is more than simply a way to make coffee; it is an entire coffee cuisine. And as espresso technology has been adopted by cultures outside Italy, that one cuisine has become many related cuisines. The components that go into these cuisines are simple, however: coffee, always brewed by the espresso method; milk (or milk substitutes); and finally various flavorings added to the drink, at one time only chocolate, but in the United States an increasing (and often bewildering) variety of syrups and garnishes.

THE THREE CUISINES

I've chosen to describe three of these cuisines: the classic northern Italian, the Italian-American, and finally, a new, thoroughly American cuisine that has erupted in many-flavored splendor out of Seattle over the past few years and will most likely come to dominate the American experience of espresso. This last tradition I'd love to dub *post-modern espresso*, but more likely names might be *Seattle-style espresso*, *cart espresso*, after the ubiquitous Seattle espresso cart, *mall espresso*, or even *latte espresso*, after the favored drink of Seattleites. I should add that Seattle, which recently has become the North American mecca of coffee culture, produces some of the purest and most elegantly presented espresso cuisine in the world. However, it also has produced its own innovating new cuisine that has about the same relationship to classic espresso as the pop singer Madonna has to her namesake.

I've described the drinks involved in the three cuisines later in this chapter. Here, however, is an overview.

The Italian Cuisine

Here the emphasis is, above all, on the coffee. There are two principal drinks: a tiny cup of straight espresso, either small, smaller, or smallest; and an austere and splendid cappuccino, the classic drink in which a single serving of fresh, exquisitely brewed espresso is topped with just enough hot milk and milk froth to allow the perfume of the coffee to penetrate every molecule of the cup. The Italian equivalent of the ubiquitous American caffè latte is the *latte macchiato*, milk "marked" or "stained" (macchiato) with espresso, much smaller than the American "latte," but similar in concept: hot milk and a little froth combined with espresso in a tall glass. Not many of these drinks are served in the average Italian bar, however, and the glass tends to hold 6 to 10 ounces, not the mammoth 16 ounces of the usual American latte glass. Caffè latte does not appear on the menus of Italian espresso bars except in places that attract American tourists. In Italian homes a drink called *caffè latte* may be made with ordinary coffee from the caffettiera and milk heated on the stove, but the perfection of the Italian bar espresso would never be ruined with the amount of hot milk the American espresso culture dumps into it. It goes without saying that the mammoth concoctions of the Seattle cuisine—double and triple servings of espresso sloshed in enough milk to satisfy a kindergarten class—are seldom if ever seen in Italian bars and caffès.

In addition to espresso drinks, Italian bars and caffès, particularly those associated with bakeries, offer an amazing hot chocolate. This is a chocolate beyond rich; it is a chocolate drinker's apocalypse. There is a saying in Italy to the effect that the hot chocolate is good only if the spoon stands up in it. This drink, if one can call it that, is often served topped with whipped cream, which makes it resemble a hot fudge sundae without the ice cream. However, a drink combining hot chocolate and espresso similar to the Italian-American *Caffè Mocha* does not appear to be offered in Italian bars and caffès. It apparently once was; one runs across references to such beverages in the Italian literature on chocolate. A writer mentions with fond nostalgia the *barbagliata* once offered in Milanese caffès, for example, and the Turinese *bicierin*, apparently both combinations of chocolate and coffee. I suspect that such drinks, together with the caffè latte, went out of style as the small, sleek espresso bar replaced the larger, more leisurely caffè after World War II, and as the espresso machine and its peculiarly Italian "less is more" aesthetic was perfected.

The Italian-American Cuisine

The Italian-American cuisine is my name for that traditional menu of espresso drinks that was developed in Italian-American communities during the 1920s through 1940s, moved from there into Bohemian and university communities via the American coffeehouse and its various offshoots during the 1950s, and by the 1960s had been taken up by the specialty coffee culture, that world of small boutique coffee roasters and burlap-decorated stores that has now grown to become a major part of the American coffee industry.

The Italian-American cuisine at first glance resembles the contemporary Italian. There are a few more choices on the menu: in particular the caffè latte and the caffè Mocha, or chocolate-espresso combination. Otherwise the list is similar: espresso; ristretto, or short espresso; cappuccino, etc. The drinks are usually larger, and the servings of espresso are definitely larger. But what sets the two cuisines apart more than anything else is the style of the coffee. In the United States, with high-quality arabica coffees cheap and widely available, espresso blends tend to be sharper and more acidy. In Italy, where the cost of coffee is higher and coffee drinkers prefer to take their espresso without milk, the emphasis is on smoother, lighter-flavored blends based on cheaper "Brazil" and robusta beans. Finally, American espresso blends, particularly on the West Coast, tend to be roasted darker than the northern Italian norm, further accentuating the more rugged flavor profile of American espressos.

Perhaps the most striking difference between the two cuisines is the rituals that surround them in public places, rituals that affect, and in turn are affected by, technical and taste factors. In Italy, every facet of the brewing and serving ritual is focused on what might be called the *perfect swallow*: The coffee is ground fresh, just before brewing; a small amount is brewed in about 25 seconds into a tiny, preheated cup; and then, before this little liquid jewel can cool or the delicate aromatics liberated by the brewing can evaporate, it is drunk, in a few rapid swallows.

Even the time it takes for a waiter or waitress to pick up an espresso and deliver it to a table probably halves the flavor potential in the cup. The premium the espresso system places on immediate consumption of the drink doubtless contributed to the trend in Italy toward the small, streamlined espresso bar that replaced the larger caffè or neighborhood bar of pre-World War II days, with its more unhurried rituals. Certainly other factors predominated in this development, including the rising cost of real estate and the faster pace of life after the war. Nevertheless, the new Gaggia brewing system introduced in the 1950s pointed to drinking the coffee immediately and quickly, to take full advantage of the extraordinary flavor perfumes liberated by the new machines, thus doubtless assisting in the postwar triumph of bar over caffè.

By comparison, the Italian-American cuisine was developed and continues to thrive in a much more leisurely context. The American customers' favorite drinks tend to be those that combine hot, frothed milk with the espresso coffee, so a serving lag between brewing and drinking is less important. These same customers for years were primarily artists, Bohemians, university students, professionals with irregular work schedules, etc., all of whom paid not only for an espresso beverage, but for the use of a table as well, where they were free to read a newspaper, write a poem, work on a term paper, or chat with a client in a comfortable and (depending on the social context) either defiantly funky or nostalgically European atmosphere.

Think as well about the fundamental tradition of American coffee drinking: the expectation of the "bottomless cup," the tradition of sipping relatively weak, often stale coffee for hours on end while one eats, works, or talks. Contrast that ritual with the one developed in the Italian espresso bar, where customers stop everything for a few moments to take three or four explosively flavorful swallows of coffee, then immediately return to work or play, riding the resonance of flavor and stimulation. The moment an Italian takes his or her espresso is a brief but utterly private moment, however public in context; you can tell by the eyes that it is a moment of silent communion between soul and coffee. Then the cup is returned to the saucer or the saucer to the counter, decisively, with a single clack, like an exclamation point, signaling the vigorous return of the soul to whatever worldly matters face it.

Once an Italian picks up an espresso cup, it stays in hand until the little pool of frothy elixir is completely consumed. By contrast, we Americans like to wrap ourselves around our coffee, nurse it, sip it, psychologically bathe in it. Thus it's no wonder that the Italian-American cuisine is longer and taller and milkier, with the same drinks, but stretched out, with more milk, and more, and more rugged-tasting coffee.

The Seattle Cuisine

The same expansive tendency is even more spectacularly in evidence in the post-modern Seattle cuisine, where one can order a triple serving of espresso in a *mondo*, or milk-shake-sized container of hot frothed milk, perhaps further enriched by a shot of mint syrup and several kinds of garnishes. When one studies the rituals of the new Seattle cuisine, however, additional differences from the traditional Italian and Italian-American cuisines emerge. If the small, standup bar is the quintessential Italian setting for espresso cuisine, and the café, with tables, chairs, newspapers, and light foods is the typical setting for the Italian-American cuisine, then the espresso cart is the characteristic setting for the Seattle cuisine.

With the espresso cart the cup, saucer, and glass have been dispensed with and replaced by a disposable cup, either Styrofoam or paper. The customers range from those types who also inhabit the traditional café—the newspaper readers, two-hour talkers, and poetry writers—to professionals and clerks who are taking their coffee break outside and on the run, rather than inside, in the office lounge or at their desk. Everything tends to be improvised and casual, and the social space around the cart is continually created and recreated by those who stand, sit, stroll, or dash back to work balancing 16 ounces of espresso drink atop a pile of manila file folders. In some ways, the carts resemble Italian espresso bars, but the customers usually walk away with their tall, milky drinks, rather than down them immediately with an elbow on the bar.

As for the Seattle cuisine itself, it represents the expansive, defiantly non-traditional, and individualistically improvising spirit of Western America at its iconoclastic best. It is a cuisine of extremes, from tall, milky, weak drinks in which the espresso can barely be detected amid the pop seductions of pomegranate or pineapple-coconut syrup to austerely macho "triples" of straight espresso;

from the nonfat latte made with decaffeinated coffee (dubbed the *Skinny No-Fun* by some espresso carts) to a *double breve*, which delivers to the non-believer's tummy two servings of caffeine and all the butterfat floating around in 12 ounces of half-and-half .

I suspect that with the development of the Seattle cuisine, with its vigorous pop interpretations of traditional drinks coupled with a sophisticated grasp of espresso technique, espresso in America has finally departed the elitist preserve of imitation Europeans, fancy food freaks, university students, artists, and urban professionals, and is on its way into the mainstream of American life.

THE CAFFÈ CUISINES IN DETAIL

What follows is a description of the various beverages that make up the espresso cuisines of the United States and Northern Italy. Although I've added a few words on the complex and interesting Latin American espresso cuisines and their North American offshoots on pages 41–42, I have chosen not to include Latin American espresso terms here for reasons of space and coherence.

For a detailed discussion of assembling the espresso cuisine in the home, see Chapter 9 and related Espresso Breaks. For advice on choosing espresso coffees, see Chapter 6.

The Classic Drinks

Espresso. One half (Italy) to two thirds (United States) of a demitasse of espresso coffee, or 1 to 2 ounces, black, usually drunk with sugar.

Caffè latte

Latte macchiato

Caffè Mocha

Cappuccino

Espresso

The five principal drinks of the classic Italian-American espresso cuisine. Clockwise, from the bottom: espresso, in three-once cup properly half-filled with rich, crema-topped coffee; caffè Mocha, in 6-ounce mug, as it was originally served in Italian-American caffès of the 1950s and 60s; caffè latte in 16-ounce glass; latte macchiato in 10-ounce glass; and the classic cappuccino in 6-ounce cup.

Espresso Romano (United States; Italian-American). Espresso served with a twist or thin slice of lemon on the side.

Espresso Ristretto, Ristretto (United States), **Corto** (Italy), **Short, Short Pull** (Pacific Northwest). "Restricted" or short (*corto*) espresso. Carries the "small is beautiful" espresso philosophy to its ultimate: The flow of espresso is cut short at about 1 ounce or one third of a demitasse (Italy) to 1 ½ ounces or one half of a demitasse (United States), producing an even denser, more perfumy cup of espresso than the norm.

Espresso Lungo, Lungo (Italy, United States), **Long, Long Pull** (Pacific Northwest). A "long" espresso, filling about two thirds or more of a demitasse. A term not

(continued on page 43)

ESPRESSO AND "EL GUSTO LATINO"

Today the espresso machine is found not only in upscale professional and student and artist hangouts, but in other, less celebrated North American neighborhoods as well, neighborhoods where few tourists and food aficionados tread.

Cubans, Brazilians, and other Latin American cultures enjoy espresso traditions that may predate the North American-Italian tradition, or at least were developed around the same time, and wherever Cubans in particular have settled in any numbers they have brought with them their own style of espresso culture.

If you do find Cuban-style espresso being served, much will be familiar: the little white cups half filled with dark coffee, the espresso machine behind the counter. But if you observe the ritual and taste the coffee, you may note some subtle differences. The little cups of black coffee are invariably served backed by glasses of cold water, and the coffee displays a dark, bitter bite gotten by roasting the beans slower and longer than the Italian or the North American norm. Although the coffee is usually drunk sweetened to the limit of possibility, it is seldom mixed with milk.

Such small cups of strong, dark-roasted, filtered coffee have been enjoyed for generations in Latin America, beginning long before the development of espresso technology. In early twentieth-century Cuba, for example, the coffee was brewed by the cold water method. A large amount of dark-roasted, finely ground coffee was steeped in relatively small amounts of cold water for several hours. The resulting concentrated but mild-tasting coffee was then filtered through cotton cloth, stored, and when needed, heated and poured into small cups half filled with sugar. The coffee was always served with glasses of chilled water, seldom if ever mixed with milk, and taken in small quantities often throughout the day, just as Italians today take their espresso.

Before the development of the espresso machine a very similar coffee tradition prevailed in Brazil and many other regions of Latin America, although the concentrated coffee was often mixed with hot milk in the morning, and the concentrate itself might be brewed by hot water as well as by cold water methods. In Ecuador restaurants and cafés deliver cold-brewed concentrate in little soy sauce dispensers, to be added to taste to either hot milk (*con leche*) or hot water (*con agua caliente*).

Obviously, the espresso method was made to order for such traditions, and it entered the mainstream of many Latin American coffee cultures long before it came into vogue in North America. It wasn't until North Americans discovered the milkier side of the Italian cuisine, the ingratiatingly dessert-like cappuccino and caffè latte, that espresso began its spread into the mainstream of coffee culture in the United States and English-speaking Canada.

The Latin Taste at Home

Unless you live in Miami or some other city with a relatively large Cuban community, you may not have an opportunity to enjoy the public side of the Latin espresso tradition. However, the Latin taste in espresso can be easily experienced at home. Markets in Latin-American neighborhoods usually carry a range of excellent pre-ground, packaged espresso coffees in the dark-roast, Latin style. These coffees constitute one of the great uncelebrated pleasures of North American espresso cuisine. They differ both from North American canned espressos, which tend to be lighter in roast and more acidy, and the packaged, pre-ground espressos imported from northern Italy, which are smoother and milder than either Latin or mainstream North American blends. The Latin espresso blends are particularly effective for large, milky drinks like the caffè latte, since Italian and mainstream North American packaged espressos may be too mild-tasting to power through the milk.

Latin espresso blends usually carry the tag "Para el gusto Latino" ("For the Latin taste") somewhere on the package. They almost always are precision-ground for good espresso brewing. The same roaster often offers more than one blend, with a variety of names and packaging. These blends may differ subtly in flavor, but their differences are usually not described in the copy on the bags. A rule of thumb: the darker the colors on the package and the more prominent the rubric "Para el Gusto Latino," the longer the coffee has been roasted, and the more characteristically Latin the flavor.

much used in the United States, since most American espresso servings are usually already "long" by Italian standards.

Espresso Con Panna, Con Panna. A single or double serving of espresso topped with whipped cream in a 6-ounce cup, usually topped by a dash of unsweetened chocolate powder.

Double Espresso (United States), **Doppio Espresso** (Italy). Double serving, or about 3 ounces (Italy) to 4 to 6 ounces (United States) of straight espresso, made with twice the amount of ground coffee as a single serving.

Cappuccino. One serving (about 1 1/2 ounces in Italy, 2 ounces in the United States) of espresso, topped by hot milk and froth. In the classic Italian-American cuisine, a good cappuccino consists of about one-third espresso, one-third milk, and about one-third rather stiff foam, in a heavy 6-ounce cup. In Italy, the milk is not frothed as thoroughly as in the United States and is presented as a heavier, soupy foam that picks up and combines with the espresso, rather than floating on top of it, as is often the case with the lighter, drier froth typical of American production. The hot, frothed milk is always added *to* the coffee in the cappuccino. Like most espresso drinks, the cappuccino is usually drunk with sugar.

This popular drink is often customized, both in the United States and in Italy. It is not unusual to hear an Italian order a cappuccino "*senza spuma*" (without froth), and at some Seattle espresso carts people often order a "dry" cappuccino, meaning a cappuccino with mostly froth and little milk.

In less sophisticated American caffès and restaurants a cappuccino can be almost anything, from what in Italy would be a weak latte macchiato to astounding concoctions in which the coffee is so thin and overextracted that it tastes like a solution of burned rubber, the milk is nearly boiled, and the froth is as stiff as overcooked meringue.

Caffè Latte, Latte (United States). In the United States, a serving of espresso and about three times as much hot milk, in a 10- to 16-ounce bowl or wide-mouthed glass, topped with a short head of froth. Caffè latte has a greater proportion of milk to coffee than a cappuccino does, and tastes weaker and milkier. Strictly speaking, the milk and coffee should be poured simultaneously, from either side of the bowl or glass.

Such combinations of hot milk and coffee have long been the favored breakfast drink of southern Europeans, although the term *caffè latte* itself appears to be little used in Italy, where those who want a breakfast coffee with more milk than froth usually order a latte macchiato, or perhaps a cappuccino without foam, *senza spuma*. In fact, in Italy a sure way to reveal that you are an American is to order a cappuccino after lunch, or a caffè latte at any time. In the United States, caffès often distinguish between caffè latte (made with espresso) and café au lait, which substitutes ordinary American filter coffee for the espresso.

Espresso Macchiato, Macchiato. A serving of espresso "stained" (macchiato) with a small quantity of hot, frothed milk. Served in the usual espresso demitasse.

Latte Macchiato. A glass filled with hot frothed milk, into which a serving of espresso has been slowly dribbled. The coffee colors, or stains, the milk. In both Italy and the

United States, this drink is presented with a relatively short head of foam. Note that in the cappuccino, the milk and froth are added to the coffee; in the caffè latte they are poured simultaneously into a large bowl or glass, mixing them, while in the latte macchiato, the espresso is poured into the milk and froth, creating a layered effect as viewed through the serving glass.

Caffè Mocha, Mocha (United States), ***Moccaccino*** (East Coast United States). Not to be confused with Mocha Java, a traditional American-roasted blend of Mocha and Java coffees. In the classic Italian-American espresso cuisine a caffè Mocha is one serving (1 1/2 to 2 ounces) of espresso, mixed with about 2 ounces of very strong hot chocolate, topped with hot frothed milk. The milk is added last, and the whole thing is usually served in an 8-ounce mug. With a classic Mocha the hot chocolate is made very strong so it can hold its own against the espresso and milk. With increasing frequency American caffès simply add chocolate fountain syrup to a caffè latte and call it a *Mocha*. So be it. The Mocha does not appear on Italian espresso menus, although the drink is probably based on various coffee-chocolate drinks once popular in Northern Italy.

Garnishes and Whipped Cream. In both the Italian and classic Italian-American cuisines, the froth of the cappuccino is garnished with a dash of unsweetened cocoa, which adds a subtle chocolate perfume to the drink. Don't be intimidated by provincial purists who claim chocolate on a cappuccino is unsophisticated; they haven't been to Italy. Some American establishments use cinnamon as well, which is definitely not done in Italy. I don't care for cinnamon on a cappuccino; I find the flavor too sharp and out of harmony with the dark tones of the coffee. The same with nutmeg. The recent practice emerging from Seattle of garnishing with a vanilla-flavored powder may not be classic, but it tastes good. Straight espresso is delicious with whipped cream (*con panna* in Italy), but topping a good, frothy cappuccino with whipped cream is as pointless as putting catsup on red-sauced spaghetti.

Post-Modern Espresso, or America Embraces the Machine

Americans have begun to subject the classic espresso cuisine to their own brand of cultural innovation. In general, it would seem that we are frustrated by the brevity and simplicity of the classic Italian and Italian-American cuisines, and want bigger drinks with more in them. Perhaps an ounce and a half of coffee in a tiny cup does fail to comfort in the middle of the Great Plains or atop the World Trade Towers. Still, I think it would be better if Americans understood and experienced the intensity and understated perfection of the classic espresso cuisines before immediately expanding them, watering them down, or adding flavored syrups and ice to them. At any rate, here are some of the more honorable results of American espresso cuisine innovation.

The majority of these creations appear to have originated in Seattle, where a passion for Italian coffee and a shortage of actual Italians seem to have fueled a veritable orgy of homegrown espresso creativity.

(continued on page 46)

ESPRESSO MACHISMO

In the U.S., espresso cuisine is often associated with the effete urbanite, the quiche-eaters and kiwi-slicers whom comedians and cartoonists so love to skewer. There is a macho side to espresso culture, however. The same swagger with which some Americans swallow live oysters, drink martinis straight up, and gobble dishes containing raw beef leads them to the straight shot of espresso as the most appropriate expression of their personal power stance. In the San Francisco area at least, one often sees men in business suits and women in Dianne Feinstein outfits cutting their way through motley gatherings of cappuccino sippers and latte bibbers to define their positions by ordering double straight espressos.

Cartoonist Gary Larson has had some fun juxtaposing traditional symbols of American macho culture and the effete associations of espresso. "Latte, Jed?" asks a seedy cowpoke, hospitably extending a Rube-Goldbergesque chuckwagon espresso pot to his sidekick. Or we share an intimate moment with "Carl (Javahead) Jones and his chopped espresso maker," the countertop espresso maker decorated with flames and Carl wearing a T-shirt with the slogan "Born to be Wired." Still, in Larson's hometown of Seattle, the fiction is often a reality. In the semirural towns north of Seattle, it is not unusual to see pickup trucks rumbling up to roadside espresso stands to pick up a double cappuccino on the way to the woods for some deer hunting or tree topping.

Of course the cup of strong black coffee has always held an important place in American male mythology. As many historians have pointed out, coffee was adopted by Americans as their national drink in part in rebellion against the tea-drinking English. The only beverage that Tarzan (a Western American hero if there ever was one, despite his gussied-up English ancestry) would touch was "an occasional cup of plain black coffee." Chuckwagon or "cowboy" coffee, in which the grounds are never taken out of the pot until they reach the lid, is a familiar part of Western American myth. It may be that espresso machismo is simply an urban extension of these myths of plain folks, strong coffee, and tall, silent men.

In Italy, of course, aspects of male swagger have long been associated with espresso. Certainly the popularity of the "short" espresso, in which an exceptionally strong, perfumy espresso barely covers the bottom of a demitasse, reflects a sort of sophisticated macho purism. It is uncanny at times to observe the similarity between the gestures of Italian men ordering and drinking espresso and the classic gestures of the American Westerner strolling up to the bar for his beer or whiskey.

Americano. A single serving of espresso with hot water added to fill a 6-ounce cup; apparently a Seattle innovation. Note that simply running 6 ounces of hot water through a single dose of ground coffee will *not* produce an Americano but will produce 6 ounces of thin, bitter, overextracted espresso. The Americano allows a regular serving of espresso to preserve its integrity and perfume, while stretching it to 6 ounces by adding the hot water.

Double Cappuccino (or double cap, pronounced partly through the nose, as in "baseball cap"). If this innovation is made correctly, you should get about 3 ounces of uncompromised espresso, brewed with double the usual amount of ground coffee, topped with 3 to 5 ounces of hot milk and froth, with emphasis on the froth. Usually served in an 8- to 10-ounce cup or mug. If the ground coffee is not doubled, and the operator simply forces twice as much water through one serving's worth of ground coffee, you're getting a bitter, watery perversion rather than a taller, stronger version of a good drink.

Triple Cappuccino. Simply three cappuccinos, usually served in a 12-ounce mug or 16-ounce glass, made with three doses of ground coffee. On behalf of the medical establishment, I should point out that this drink is probably not good for one's health.

Double Caffè Latte. The amount of ground coffee is doubled and the amount of coffee brewed is doubled. This drink is almost always served in a 16-ounce glass. As with the single caffè latte, the head of froth is modest and the drink stronger than a single caffè latte but still relatively milky.

Triple Caffè Latte. See above. Simply a very strong caffè latte, made with three servings of espresso brewed with a triple dose of ground coffee, together with enough hot milk and froth to fill a 16-ounce glass.

Mocha Latte. A taller, milkier version of the classic Mocha (see page 44). If I were to suggest proportions for this invention, they would be one part properly strong espresso, one part properly strong chocolate, and three parts milk and froth. These proportions produce a drink that is milkier, taller, and more muted than the classic Mocha but still rich enough to satisfy.

White Chocolate Mocha, Bianco Mocha. A caffè Mocha (see page 44) made with white chocolate. Sweet white baking chocolate is melted in a double boiler, combined with milk, and used in place of the normal chocolate concentrate in the caffè Mocha. Apparently Berkeley, not Seattle, gave birth to this sweet, delicate version of the classic drink.

Café Au Lait. In some American cafés, a drink made with about half American-roast filter coffee and about half hot milk and froth, usually served in a 12- or 16-ounce glass or bowl. The proportion of coffee to milk has to be larger than with the espresso-based caffè latte because American filter coffee is so delicate in flavor and light in body compared to espresso.

Iced Espresso. This is usually a double espresso, poured over plenty of crushed, not cubed, ice, in a smallish fancy glass. Some caffès top the iced coffee with whipped cream. Caffès that brew and refrigerate a pitcher of espresso in advance when they feel a hot morning on the way fail to deliver the brewed-fresh perfume of true espresso, but the practice still makes a fine drink, one that doesn't need to be iced and diluted as much as the version made with fresh espresso.

Iced Cappuccino. Best made with a single or double serving of freshly brewed espresso poured over crushed ice, topped with an ounce or two of cold milk, then some froth (not hot milk) from the machine to top it off. This drink should always be served in a glass. The triple contrast of coffee, milk, and froth, all bubbling around the ice, makes a pleasant sight on a hot day.

Espresso Granita. This is originally an Italian specialty but has been adapted in the United States in ways that make it decadently American. Traditional Italian *granitas* usually involved freezing strong, unsweetened or lightly sweetened espresso, crushing it, and serving it in a parfait glass or sundae dish topped with lightly sweetened whipped cream. The latest American version blends espresso, milk, and ample sugar, and freezes the combination in special dispensing machines. It's called a *granita latte* in Seattle, where it apparently originated. The granita latte is a nice summer experience, particularly if it's made with caffè-brewed espresso rather than with somebody else's espresso flavoring.

Breve. Seattle-originated term for a caffè latte made with frothed half-and-half.

Flavored Caffè Latte. The Seattle cuisine's most ubiquitous innovation is the flavored latte, in which a (usually impeccably made) caffè latte is transformed into a chocolate-mint latte, grenadine latte, cherry latte, or any number of other lattes, each through the addition of a dollop of the relevant Italian-style fountain syrup.

The flavored caffè latte, made correctly (about 1/2 to 1 ounce of syrup to every serving of espresso and approximately 8 ounces of hot milk), should strike a judicious balance between the milk-muted bite of the espresso and the seduction of the syrup. Syrup manufacturers usually recommend stirring the syrup into the milk while frothing, but for reasons of economy and convenience most caffès add the syrup after the milk has been frothed and poured.

Eggnog Latte. Seattleites and their fellow celebrants around the world toast the holiday season with this combination of espresso and hot frothed eggnog.

Flavored Frothed Milk, Steamer, Moo. Essentially, a flavored caffè latte without the espresso. One-half to 1 ounce of Italian-style syrup flavoring in about 8 ounces of hot frothed milk, served with a modest head of froth in a caffè latte glass.

The Latte Meets the Soda Fountain, or Syrup-Oriented Variations. These are further elaborations on the flavored caffè latte, and may involve ice cream or whipped cream (often flavored with Italian-style syrups), topped with everything from maraschino cherries to nuts and M&Ms—all in addition to the flavored frothed milk (and yes, the espresso is in there somewhere). Since the budding North American espresso cart industry encourages new entrepreneurs to distinguish themselves from their competition by pioneering novel espresso concoctions, we can expect ever more extravagant inventions along these feverishly creative lines. Some of us would prefer espresso carts to distinguish themselves with flawless espresso and perfect cappuccino, but we're probably the same killjoys who order vanilla ice cream when we could get Cherry Garcia. For suggestions on exploring the soda-fountain espresso cuisine at home, see pages 144 and 150.

The Latte Meets the Health Bar, or Health-Oriented Variations. All over the United States, and particularly in Seattle, any number of custom variations are carried out on the classic drinks, particularly the caffè latte, all designed to mute the presumed health hazards presented by the classic cuisine. Drinks are made with nonfat milk, with 1 percent milk, with 2 percent milk, and with soy milk. They are also made with decaffeinated coffee and with various coffee substitutes. *Café Olé* magazine, the informative and often amusing voice of the Seattle coffee culture, informs us that the following jargon prevails at many Seattle espresso carts: *Tall Skinny,* a tall caffè latte made with nonfat or 1 percent milk; *Tall Two,* a tall caffè latte made with 2 percent milk; *Niente* or *Why Bother,* a cappuccino made with decaffeinated coffee and non-fat milk; *No Fun,* a caffè latte assembled with decaffeinated espresso; and *Double No Fun,* same as the preceding with a double serving of decaffeinated espresso.

THE ROAST

Espresso Breaks

Coffee Roasts
Roasting Your Own

Roasting is the key to the transformation of a green seed into a rich, complex beverage. Nothing affects coffee flavor more than how the beans have been roasted. The flavor nuances imparted to coffee by roasting are particularly important in espresso cuisine, because the dark styles of roast used in espresso tend to mute taste characteristics inherent in the bean itself and replace them with characteristics generated by the roast.

ROASTING CHEMISTRY

The green coffee bean, like all the other nuts, kernels, and beans we consume, is composed of fats, proteins, fiber, and miscellaneous chemical compounds. The aroma and flavor that make coffee so distinctive are present only potentially until the heat of roasting simultaneously forces much of the moisture out of the bean and draws out of the base matter of the bean fragrant little beads of a volatile, oily substance variously called *coffee essence*, *coffee oil*, or *coffeol*. This substance is not properly an oil, since it (fortunately) dissolves in water. It also evaporates easily, readily absorbs other less desirable flavors, and generally proves to be as fragile a substance as it is tasty. Without it, there's no coffee, only sour brown water and caffeine; yet it constitutes only one two-hundredth of the weight of the bean.

The roasted bean is, in a sense, simply a dry package for this oil. In medium- or American-roast coffee, the oil gathers in little pockets throughout the heart of the bean.

As the bean is held in the roaster for longer periods or at higher temperatures, as it is with darker roasts used in the espresso cuisine, more moisture is lost, and the oil develops further and begins to rise to the surface of the bean, giving darker-roasted beans their characteristic oily appearance. Beneath the oil, the hard matter of the bean begins to contribute the slightly bitter flavor characteristic of the darkest roasts of coffees. Eventually, the bean turns to near charcoal and tastes definitively burned; this ultimately roasted coffee, variously called *dark French*, *heavy roast*, *Neapolitan*, or occasionally *Italian*, has an unmistakable charcoal tang.

Dark roasts also contain considerably less acid and somewhat less caffeine than lighter roasts; these substances go up the chimney with the roasting smoke. Consequently, dark roasts used in the espresso cuisine display less of the dry snap or bite coffee people call *acidy* (see page 62).

ROAST TERMINOLOGY

The common terms for roasts among most coffee sellers are the standard *American* or *medium* roast (medium brown in color; bright and acidy tasting); *Viennese*, *light French*, or *full city* (slightly darker in color than American; smoother and less acidy with the merest undertone of dark bittersweetness); *Italian*, *espresso*, or *continental* (dark brown in color, with oily patches on the surface of the bean; only the slightest acidy tones, with the bittersweet tang distinct); *Italian*, *espresso*, or *French* (very dark

(continued on page 53)

ESPRESSO BREAK

COFFEE ROASTS

Attaching names to coffee roasts is one of those exercises in communication that is as futile as it is necessary. Exactly at what point does drizzle become rain? When does light French roast become Italian roast? One roaster's terminology may be totally different from another's, and in an absolute sense, there are as many shades and nuances of roast as there are batches of coffee that emerge from a roasting machine.

Given that pessimistic introduction, I here present most of the names used in the United States to describe styles of roast, arranged so as to roughly correspond to descriptions of the appearance of the beans and associated taste characteristics. See chart on page 52. The numbered categories are my invention and are intended to help make sense of the polyglot list of names by dividing them into roughly related groups according to the style of roast to which they refer. Some names appear in more than one category; such overlap is necessary because one roaster's *French* may be another one's *Italian*. No one name appears in more than two adjacent categories, however, so we are not facing complete anarchy.

Categories 3 through 5 all describe roasts suitable for espresso; choosing from among them is a matter of personal taste.

Also be reminded that the taste of a roast is influenced by the origin or blend of the green beans subject to the roasting (see Chapters 5 and 6) and by the length and temperature of the roast (coffees brought to a dark roast more slowly, at lower temperatures, usually display a sharper flavor and less oil on the surface of the bean than do coffees brought to the same roast color more quickly, at higher temperatures).

Coffee Roasts: Names, Colors, Taste

1	Light brown; dry surface.	Cinnamon New England Light	Tastes more like toasted grain than coffee, with distinct acidy tones.
2	Medium brown; dry surface.	Regular American Medium-high Medium Brown	For an American, the characteristic coffee flavor. The grain taste is gone; the acidy sharpness is richer and more rounded than in category 1.
3	Slightly darker brown; faint patches of oil on the surface.	Full City City High Viennese* Light French Velvet	A slight dark-roasted, bittersweet tang is present but almost indistinguishable. Less acidy snap than category 2; generally a more rounded flavor.
4	Dark brown; distinctly oily surface.	Italian Espresso European French After-dinner Continental Dark	A definite bittersweet tang; all acidy tones gone.
5	Darker brown; distinct patches of oil on the surface.	Espresso Italian Light Italian After-dinner Continental Dark	A definite bittersweet tang; some very muted acidy tones remain.
6	Very dark brown, almost black; very shiny, oily surface.	Dark French French Italian Neapolitan Spanish Heavy	Burned or charcoal tones plus the bittersweet tang with an emphasis on the bitter; all acidy tones gone. Thinner bodied than 2 through 5.

*Viennese also sometimes refers to a blend of about one-third dark-roasted beans (4 or 5) and about two-thirds medium-roasted beans (2 or 3).

brown in color; surface of the bean covered with oil; all acidy notes gone and the bittersweetness dominant); and *French*, *dark French*, or *Neapolitan* (nearly black in color; very oily surface; charcoal or burned tones dominate; thin-bodied in the cup).

Of course, the "standard" medium roast varies greatly by region and by roaster. The West Coast generally prefers a darker standard than the East Coast, with the Midwest appropriately somewhere between. As for roasters, all vary the roast slightly to bring out what they regard as the unique characteristics of each coffee, but this perfect moment varies according to the philosophy of the roaster. To roasters who adhere to the dark end of the spectrum, lighter-roasted coffees taste too acidy and almost sour; to those who adhere to the light end, darker-roasted coffees taste muted or charred.

Roasting Philosophy and Espresso

A similar difference in philosophy prevails among roasters in regard to espresso coffees. Some prefer to roast their espresso blends less darkly, some more. Some prefer to stop the roasting at the point where the acidy tones of the coffee are still discernible and the dark-roasted bitter-sweetness is just beginning to develop, with only patches of oil flecking the still dry surface of the bean. Others prefer a darker roast in which the characteristic bitter-sweetness of the dark roast completely dominates any remaining acidy tones, and the bean is distinctly dark brown in color and shiny with oil.

Your best bet is to learn to associate flavor with the

A drum roaster of the kind often used in smaller specialty coffee-roasting establishments.

color and appearance of the bean rather than with name alone, but for reference almost everything you need to know about the names of roasts is condensed in chart form on page 52, with the roast styles used in espresso cuisine indicated.

ONLY BY TASTING

Only by tasting a variety of dark-roasted blends from a variety of coffee roasters can you determine whether you prefer your espresso coffee roasted in a style that leans toward the lighter end of the espresso spectrum, with some of the acidy notes still discernible (category 4 on page 52), or toward the darker end, where the bitter-sweet tones completely dominate (category 5). You may even find that you prefer a distinctly acidy style (category 3), or (particularly if you liked the coffee you tasted in northern France) a very dark, almost black, charred-tasting style (category 6).

Your choice will be complicated in terms of roast because the different blends of beans being roasted will bring different flavor characteristics to the roast. For more information on beans and blending see page 87. Again, all you can do is taste and experiment. A final factor that complicates discussion of the flavor characteristics of various roasts is that coffees brought to a dark roast more slowly, at lower temperatures, usually display a sharper flavor and less oil on the surface of the bean than do coffees brought to the same roast color more quickly, at higher temperatures. In this slower style of roast, preferred by many traditional Latin espresso drinkers, the oil tends to bake on the surface of the bean, which gives the bean a dark yet dry appearance and an almost smoky sharpness in the cup attractive to those who value the taste.

The most fastidious of roasters roasts each component of a blend separately, to bring out what the roaster feels are the best qualities each coffee can bring to the total blend. Some blends of roast may display a dramatic visual contrast between lighter- and darker-roasted beans, but with others the modulations in color and roast among the components of the blend may be so subtle as to be barely discernible.

ROASTING YOUR OWN

Home coffee roasting is a simple procedure with a wide margin for error. It provides the espresso aficionado with several advantages: fresher coffee, less expensive coffee, and above all the opportunity to make unlimited personal experiments with roast and blend.

Requirements for Roasting

The physical requirements for roasting coffee are simple: The coffee needs to be evenly exposed to air temperatures of at least 400° F for five to ten minutes and must be cooled at the right moment. The main challenges of home roasting are how to keep the beans from roasting unevenly and when to stop the roast.

There are almost as many ways to home-roast coffee as there are to cook meat or vegetables, but the following two methods offer the home roaster maximum control over the process.

Home Roasting in the Oven

In this method a thin layer of green beans is spread evenly over a perforated surface in an ordinary kitchen oven, allowing the convection currents of the oven to flow through the beans and maintain a reasonably even roast.

For the perforated surface use an ordinary vegetable steamer, the kind that has petal-like edges and expands to fit inside a pot. You can roast about three ounces of beans at a time in a single steamer. If you want to roast a half-pound of coffee in one session, you need three of these steamers.

You also need an ordinary oven (not a microwave), a kitchen timer, a supply of green beans, and a small sample of beans that have been commercially roasted to the style you prefer. A strong kitchen fan or easy access to a patio or back porch also helps, since the cooling beans emit a pungent, persistent smoke.

Preheat the oven to about 425° F (no lower). Place the green coffee beans in the perforated inserts, spreading them evenly across the bottom and up the opened sides, about two beans deep. Place the inserts in the oven and set the kitchen timer for 10 minutes (a minute or two less if you have preheated oven higher than 425° F). Place the sample beans near the oven, to use for color comparison.

Soon you will hear the beans crackling, which indicates that the release of bound moisture and the development of the coffee oil has begun. A pungent odor—the smell of the roasting smoke—may escape from around the oven door. The crackling will continue. In about ten minutes from the start of roasting, or about one to two minutes after the crackling begins, check the color of the beans. Open the oven door as briefly as possible. Continue to check every one to two minutes until the beans in the oven have achieved a slightly lighter shade than the color of the sample.

Immediately remove the beans from the oven and place them under the kitchen fan or outside on a back porch or patio. The beans will continue to roast from their internal heat for a couple of minutes, which is why you should be careful to remove them from the oven before they achieve the full color you desire. Don't be alarmed if your roast is slightly scorched or more darkly roasted in some places than in others. It should still taste much better than partly staled, store-bought coffee. In subsequent roastings, experiment with timing until you achieve the exact style of roast you desire.

Home Roasting Using a Small Electric Home Roaster

Several small home electric roasting devices have been marketed over the past few years. All work on the same *fluid bed* principle: the beans are simultaneously heated and agitated by a powerful column of hot air, much like small electric popcorn poppers heat and agitate popping corn.

The best of these devices have a glass roasting chamber enabling you to observe the changing color of the beans; a chaff collector at the top of the roasting chamber, to prevent the chaff from blowing around the kitchen; and an automatic timer, permitting you to set the number of minutes you wish to roast the beans before the cooling cycle is triggered. Simpler versions of the home fluid-bed roaster may ask you to take more immediate control over the operation by timing the roast yourself by monitoring bean temperature or color. All home fluid-bed roasters provide a means to quench the roast with cool air, however, which is the most useful feature of these devices.

Home electric roasters come with instructions. Keep in mind, however, that the "normal" roast cited in the instructions will be lighter in style than the roasts used in the espresso cuisine, so you may need to experiment with longer roasting times.

For this method you need a supply of green coffee beans, a small sample of beans that have been commercially roasted to the color and style you prefer, and the home electric roasting device with accompanying instructions. Again, coffee roasting produces a smoke that is pleasant-smelling at first but soon becomes cloying, so you should plan to do your roasting either outdoors on porch or patio or under a strong kitchen fan. Most small home roasters incorporate filters or screens that prevent chaff from blowing around the kitchen, but these devices do little to contain roasting smoke.

Place the measure of beans recommended by the manufacturer in the roasting chamber. *Use neither more nor fewer beans than recommended in the instructions*; too many beans will not agitate properly and will roast unevenly; too few beans will bounce wildly around the chamber, both roasting improperly and breaking apart during the last phases of the cycle.

For classic espresso cuisine plan to roast for about two minutes longer than the manufacturer recommends for a "normal" roast, and stand by, with your sample beans available for inspection next to the roaster.

When the beans inside the chamber reach a color *slightly lighter* than your sample beans, either switch on the cooling cycle or advance the timer manually to the position that initiates the cooling cycle. If your roaster does incorporate a timer, make note of the setting for use in subsequent sessions. As with the oven method, you will need to experiment over several sessions to determine the timing appropriate to the exact style of roast you prefer.

Ball Roaster

Ball Roaster

Final Notes

Every coffee roasts slightly differently. Denser "hard bean" coffees grown at higher altitudes require a higher temperature and/or longer roasting time than do more porous, lower-grown coffees. Older coffees generally roast more quickly than more moist "new crop" coffees; decaffeinated coffees roast differently from untreated coffees. With every new coffee you buy, you may need to adjust the time and/or the temperature of your roast at least slightly to achieve optimum results. The most careful of espresso roasters roasts each component of a blend separately to best bring out its unique contribution to the total effect of the blend, but for home roasting you may wish to combine the coffees of your blend before roasting. See Chapter 4 for more on roasting and Chapters 5 and 6 for more on blending in the espresso cuisine.

Freshly roasted coffee is at its best if it is allowed to rest for about 24 hours after roasting, permitting the recently volatilized oils to stabilize. If you're impatient or needy, however, grind immediately and enjoy.

If you need help finding sources for roasting apparatus and green coffee beans, turn to Finding Espresso Coffee and Equipment, pages 169–170, or consult the companion volume to this one, *Coffee: A Guide to Buying, Brewing, and Enjoying.*

Common home appliances of the nineteenth century: coffee roasters designed to fit inside the burner openings of coal or wood stoves.

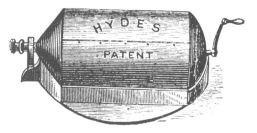

Cylinder Roaster

A COFFEE BEAN PRIMER

Espresso Breaks

Decaffeinated Coffees: The Garden Without the Snake
Organic and Other Chemical-Free Coffees

The relationship between the espresso we drink and the coffee berry as it ripens on a tree in forest or plantation is both simple and complicated. The simple part is obvious: no berry, no espresso. The complex part is everything else. Since the seed of the berry that ultimately becomes espresso is subject to so many complex processes between the moment it ripens and the moment its rich, dark infusion is finally drunk, tracing taste characteristics that appear in the cup back to the bean itself is a perilous conceptual undertaking, fraught with caveat and equivocation.

AMBIGUOUS RELATIONSHIPS

Take, for example, a quality embodied by all good espresso: heavy body, meaning a sensation of fullness in the mouth. Starting on the distant, berry end of the process, certain of the world's coffee beans definitely do produce a fuller-bodied beverage than do certain other coffee beans. High-grown coffees usually are heavier bodied than lower-grown coffees, for example; coffees of the *Coffea arabica* species generally display a fuller body than most coffees of the *Coffea robusta* species; high-quality Indonesian coffees typically exhibit a heavier body than other Pacific coffees; and so on.

Yet, does the full body of a particular cup of espresso necessarily mean the coffees that comprise it came from beans known for their heavy body? No, not really.

A properly brewed espresso is fuller-bodied than a poorly brewed espresso, for example. Furthermore, coffee roasted either relatively lightly, as in some North

American cuisine, or very darkly, as in some northern French cuisine, will produce a lighter-bodied coffee than the middle ranges of dark brown usually used for espresso. How a coffee has been processed and handled after picking also affects body. Coffees that have been subjected to decaffeination processes frequently display less body than coffees that have not been so processed, for instance. Coffees that have been held in warehouses for two or three years before roasting tend to be heavier in body than "new crop" coffees that have been roasted soon after picking. Finally, the methods by which the coffee seed has been picked, divested of its fruit, dried, cleaned, and sorted also affect body.

Does all of this complicated history mean that we must simply throw up our hands and take whatever the coffee store gives us, relinquishing our hallowed rights as consumers and obsessive connoisseurs to know what we're drinking and why? Of course not, but there are no easy answers either.

In attempting to make sense of these complexities, I would like to proceed rather systematically, first by identifying some broad taste characteristics that apply to coffee generally and espresso coffee in particular, then by describing how various factors and processes that affect the green bean influence those characteristics as they display themselves in the cup of espresso we finally drink.

PROFESSIONAL TASTING CATEGORIES

One of the most desperate acts possible in human communication is attempting to explain how something tastes

An early twentieth-century cupping room, the gustatory control center of the roasting operation. Note the small roasters on the right back wall, used to roast samples of green coffees, and the rotating tasting table, flanked by hour-glass-shaped spittoons (the coffee-cupping ritual involves sucking the coffee noisily from a spoon, swishing it about the mouth, and spitting it out). Contemporary cupping rooms differ from this one only in detail.

to someone who hasn't tasted it. Nevertheless, for commercial reasons and because we humans like to talk about experiences that give us pleasure, culture has come up with some terms for describing the various nuances that manifest in the taste of coffee.

First, here are a few terms and concepts used by coffee professionals to discuss the relative merits of various green coffees. These terms describe taste characteristics associated with the bean itself; they display themselves most clearly in coffees brought to the relatively light roast used by professionals to evaluate or "cup" coffee.

The more romantic of these tasting terms have been carried over into the prose used to sell specialty coffees; the less romantic remain the practical property of the folks who actually work in the business.

Acidity, Acidy

Acidity refers to the high, thin notes, the dryness a coffee produces at the back of the palate and under the edges of the tongue. This pleasant tartness, snap, or twist is what coffee people call *acidity*. In a poor-quality or under-roasted coffee the acidy notes can become sour and acidic rather than brisk, but in a fine, medium-roasted arabica coffee, they will be complex, rich, and vibrant. The acidy notes also carry, wrapped in their nuances, much of the distinctiveness of rare coffees.

You will not run into the terms *acidity* or *acidy* in your local coffee seller's signs and brochures. Most retailers avoid describing a coffee as acidy for fear consumers will confuse a positive acidy brightness with an unpleasant sourness. Instead you will find a variety of creative substitutes: *bright*, *dry*, *brisk*, *vibrant*, etc.

The darker the style of roast, the less distinct the acidy notes will be. In the dark brown roasts used in the espresso cuisine, the acidy notes will continue to manifest themselves, although less distinctly than in lighter roasts. When a coffee is brought to an extremely dark roast— the black, charcoal style usually called *French* or *dark French* roast—the acidy notes disappear altogether.

If you harbor questions about the effect of acidity on the taste of espresso, purchase a straight Indonesian (Sumatran, Sulawesi, or Java) coffee brought to a dark roast, and taste it against a Colombian or Kenyan coffee brought to a similar roast. A distinct dryness will gather under your tongue when you taste the Colombian or Kenyan, which in the Indonesian coffee will be replaced by a rich heaviness.

Body

Body or *mouth feel* is the sense of heaviness, richness, and thickness at the back of the tongue when the coffee is swished around the mouth. To pursue a wine analogy, burgundies and certain other red wines are heavier in body than clarets and most white wines. In this case wine and coffee tasters use the same term for a similar phenomenon.

Coffees from various parts of the world vary in body. The most celebrated coffees are usually heavy in body; the best Indonesian coffees are particularly so noted. However, as I indicated earlier, in espresso the roasting and brewing processes have considerably more effect on body than the characteristics of the original green bean. Virtually every detail of advice and prescription on brewing offered on pages 126–129 has to do with maximizing body and richness in the final cup.

Aroma

Some coffees may be more aromatic than others, and some may best display certain distinctive characteristics in their "nose," as tasters say. For example, certain East African coffees exhibit a subtle floral note that can be experienced most clearly in the aroma, particularly at the moment the crust of ground coffee is broken in the traditional tasting ritual.

Again, however, the dark-roasting involved in espresso cuisine mutes such subtleties, partly replacing them with the more general aromatics generated by the dark roast. Nearly black roasts may display little aroma of any kind except the charcoal pungency of the blackened bean,

(continued on page 69)

Decaffeinated Coffees: The Garden Without the Snake

Decaffeinated coffees have had the caffeine soaked out of them. Most specialty roasters offer a variety of decaffeinated coffees for espresso cuisine.

Coffee is decaffeinated in its green state, before the delicate oils are developed through roasting. Hundreds of patents exist for decaffeination processes, but only a few are actually used.

All decaffeination processes currently in use begin the same way: The green beans are pre-soaked in water to open their pores and "free" the bound-up caffeine. After that first step the various processes vary in their approach.

The trick is to take out the caffeine without also removing the various components that give coffee its particularly complex flavor.

Traditional or European Process

In the process variously called the *solvent process,* *European process,* *traditional process,* or *conventional process,* the caffeine removal is accomplished by first extracting both flavor components *and* caffeine from the beans by soaking them in hot water (step A in the diagram on page 64), then separating the beans and water (B), and stripping the caffeine from the flavor-laden water by means of a solvent that selectively unites with the caffeine (C). The solvent-laden caffeine is then skimmed from the surface of the water (D), and the water, now free of both caffeine and solvent, is reunited with the beans (E), which soak up the flavor components again. The beans are then dried and sold (F). The caffeine is later extracted from the solvent, by the way, and sold to makers of pharmaceuticals and soft drinks.

The solvents currently in use are methylene chloride and ethyl acetate. Methylene chloride has been associated with the depletion of the ozone layer, and is being phased out in Europe in favor of ethyl acetate. Since most specialty coffees using this process are treated in Europe, it is increasingly likely that the traditional process decaffeinated coffees at your specialty store were processed using ethyl acetate. Ethyl acetate is found naturally in fruit, so you may see coffees decaffeinated by processes making use of it called *natural process* or *naturally* decaffeinated.

Regardless of which solvent is used, note that the *solvent never touches the bean itself.* Also note that both methylene chloride and ethyl acetate evaporate very easily. Even if small amounts of solvent were returned to the bean with the hot water, it is highly unlikely that even the tiniest of residues survive the high temperatures of the roasting and brewing processes that occur before the coffee is actually drunk.

Traditional or European Process

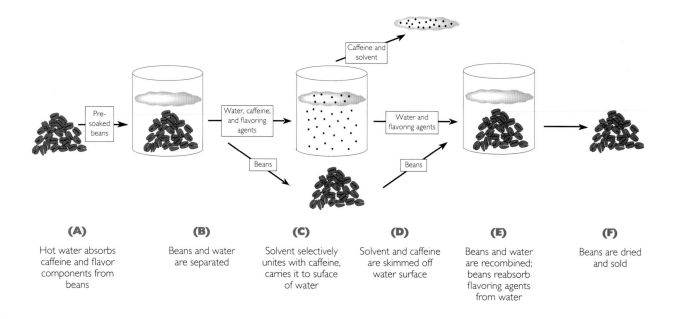

(A)	**(B)**	**(C)**	**(D)**	**(E)**	**(F)**
Hot water absorbs caffeine and flavor components from beans	Beans and water are separated	Solvent selectively unites with caffeine, carries it to suface of water	Solvent and caffeine are skimmed off water surface	Beans and water are recombined; beans reabsorb flavoring agents from water	Beans are dried and sold

Nevertheless, consumers' almost metaphysical fear of such substances has led to the commercial development of alternative processes.

Swiss-Water or Water-Only Process

There are two phases to this benign-sounding process. In the first, start-up phase (step A in the diagram on page 65), green beans are soaked in hot water, which removes both flavor components and caffeine from the beans. This first, start-up batch of beans is then discarded, while the caffeine is stripped from the water by means of activated charcoal filters, leaving the flavor components behind in the water and producing what the Swiss-Water Process people call "flavor-charged water"— water crammed full of the goodies but without the caffeine. This special water becomes the medium for the decaffeination of *subsequent* batches of green beans.

When soaked in the flavor-charged but caffeine-free water (B), new batches of beans give up their caffeine *but not their flavor components*, which remain more or less

"Swiss-Water" or Water-Only Process

(A) In the startup phase, green beans are soaked in hot water; green beans are discarded; caffeine is removed from water by charcoal filtering, resulting in a batch of flavor-charged but caffeine-free water

(B) Flavor-charged but caffeine-free water circulates through a new batch of green beans, removing caffeine only

(E) Flavor-charged but caffeine-free water is ready for next batch of green beans

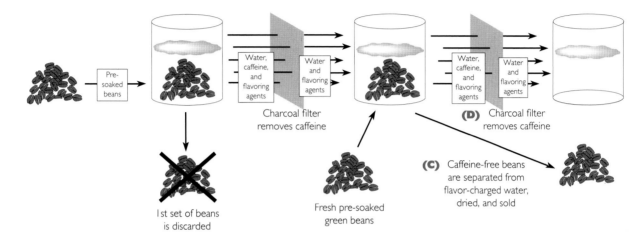

Pre-soaked beans

Water, caffeine, and flavoring agents

Water and flavoring agents

Charcoal filter removes caffeine

(D) Charcoal filter removes caffeine

1st set of beans is discarded

Fresh pre-soaked green beans

(C) Caffeine-free beans are separated from flavor-charged water, dried, and sold

intact in the bean. Apparently the water is so charged with the flavor components of the bean that it can absorb no more of them, whereas it *can* absorb the villainous caffeine.

Having thus been deprived of their caffeine but not their flavor components, the beans are then dried and sold (C), while the flavor-charged water is cleaned of its caffeine by another run through charcoal filters (D) and sent back to decaffeinate a further batch of beans (E).

The problem with this process for speciality coffee roasters is that the flavor components of various batches of beans may become a bit blurred. If your coffee is an Ethiopian, for example, and yesterday's batch was a Colombian, it may be hard to determine exactly whose flavor components actually inhabit the bean at the end of the process. Your Ethiopian may end up with a little of yesterday's Colombian in it, whereas tomorrow's Costa Rican may end up with a little of your Ethiopian, and so on.

The Swiss-Water people have various subtle ways of correcting for this problem, however, and over the years have steadily improved the quality of their product. This success, combined with the encouraging fact that no solvent whatsoever is used in the process and the reassuring ring of "Swiss-Water," with its associations of glaciers, alpine health enthusiasts, and chewy breakfast cereal, have combined to make this process the most popular of the competing decaffeination methods in the specialty coffee world.

You also may see coffees described as "French-Water Process" decaffeinated. This term does not mean that the coffees in question have been soaked in barrels of Beaujolais; it does mean that other firms are trying to horn in on the Swiss-Water Process firm's business with their own versions of the method.

Sparkling Water Process

In this method, the green beans are bathed in a combination of water and highly compressed carbon dioxide (CO_2), the same naturally occurring substance that plants consume and human beings produce. In its compressed form the carbon dioxide behaves partly like a gas and partly like a liquid, and has the property of combining selectively with the caffeine in the beans themselves.

After the beans have been pre-soaked in water to open their pores and "free" the caffeine, they are subjected to a longer soaking in compressed CO_2 and a small amount of water (step A in the diagram on the opposite page). During soaking the caffeine-laden "wet" CO_2 is continuously cycled through a second "wash" tank (B), in which additional water is run through it, stripping it of its caffeine. The renovated CO_2, drained of both excess water and caffeine, is then returned (C) to the soak tank to continue with the process of stripping the beans of their caffeine. Eventually, the caffeine-free beans are removed from the circulating liquid CO_2, dried, and sold (D).

At this writing coffees decaffeinated by the Sparkling Water method are just beginning to reach the specialty market in significant quantity. The name "Sparkling Water Process," by the way, is a publicist's inspired allusion to the fact that both this decaf-

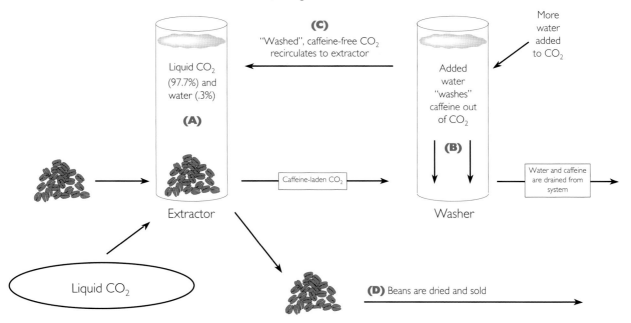

"Sparkling Water" Process

Green beans are continuously bathed in wet, liquified CO_2 for about 10 hours. CO_2 selectively dissolves caffeine, leaving flavor elements intact

(C) "Washed", caffeine-free CO_2 recirculates to extractor

More water added to CO_2

Liquid CO_2 (97.7%) and water (.3%)

(A)

Added water "washes" caffeine out of CO_2

(B)

Extractor

Caffeine-laden CO_2

Washer

Water and caffeine are drained from system

Liquid CO_2

(D) Beans are dried and sold

feination process and sparkling water make use of the same two simple ingredients: CO_2 and water.

Carbon Dioxide or CO_2 Process

Like the Sparkling Water Process, the CO_2 process uses compressed, liquid CO_2 to dissolve and selectively unite with the caffeine in the green beans. Unlike the Sparkling Water Process, however, no water is used, the beans are bathed in liquid CO_2 only, and the caffeine is stripped from the CO_2 by means of activated charcoal filters. At this writing the pure CO_2 process is used mainly to decaffeinate coffees for preground, commercial blends, so it does not figure in the world of most espresso buyers.

Caffeine, Flavor, and Decaffeination Processes

Since caffeine in itself is tasteless, coffee flavor should not be affected by its removal. However, in the process of its removal, coffee beans are subjected to considerable abuse, including prolonged soaking in hot water and/or liquid CO_2. Consequently, most caffeine-free coffees are difficult to roast, and in general display *somewhat* less body and aroma than similar untreated coffees. One can, of course, create blends of treated and untreated beans, thus cutting down on caffeine intake while maintaining full flavor and body in at least one component of the blend.

since virtually all of the delicate aromatic oils will have been burned off.

In the brewing process aroma is particularly promoted by freshness; the more recently the coffee has been roasted and ground, the more powerful the aroma. Once liberated in the cup aroma fades quickly, which is why the little cups used for espresso are preheated and the drink consumed quickly.

Finish

If aroma is the overture of the coffee, then *finish* is the resonant silence at the end of the piece. Finish is a term relatively recently brought over into coffee tasting from wine connoisseurship; it describes the aftertaste that lingers on the palate after the coffee is swallowed or (in the professional tasting ritual) spit out.

Generally, heavy-bodied coffees have longer and more resonant finishes than lighter-bodied varieties. But once again, in espresso cuisine brewing and roasting may have considerably more impact on finish than the qualities of the bean itself. Freshness in particular affects finish; a freshly roasted and ground espresso coffee will display a much more vibrant finish than coffees that have partly staled.

Flavor

Flavor is the most ambiguous of the terms defined here. Acidity has something to do with it, as do body and aroma. The following are some terms and categories used to evaluate flavor among professional tasters. Some of these terms crop up in discussions of espresso blends and coffees; others are used exclusively to describe characteristics of medium-roasted varietal coffees.

Richness. Describes an interesting, satisfying fullness.

Complexity. Complexity describes flavor that shifts among pleasurable possibilities, tantalizes, and doesn't completely reveal itself at any one moment; a harmonious multiplicity of sensation.

Balance. When tasting coffees for defects, professional tasters use the term *balance* to describe a coffee that does not localize at any one point on the palate; in other words, it is not imbalanced in the direction of some one (often undesirable) taste characteristic. As a more general term of evaluation, balance appears to mean that no one quality overwhelms all others, yet there is enough complexity in the coffee to arouse interest.

Varietal Distinction or Character. If an unblended coffee has characteristics that both set it off from other coffees, yet identify it as what it is, it has *varietal distinction*. A rich, winy acidity characterizes Yemen and many good East African coffees, for example, whereas heavy body and rich finish are distinctive characteristics of most good Sumatran coffees. Once more, the dark-roasting in the espresso cuisine mutes most varietal distinctions.

Earthiness, Wildness. These terms describe a sort of muted medicinal or gamey flavor that derives from primitive processing of the coffee fruit. It is a characteristic usually viewed as a defect, but in some contexts may be seen as a virtue. Roasters from southern Italy and those who roast for the Latin taste in the United States may include small quantities of earthy-tasting Brazilian coffees in certain of their espresso blends. The earthy taste is never allowed to dominate, however, but simply to complicate.

Flavor Defects. Many terms in the coffee trade describe dramatic flavor aberrations, most caused by careless handling of the coffee fruit. Since these terms describe characteristics that disqualify coffees from the premium market, they are irrelevant to the espresso drinker, but for the record they include *sour, harsh, grassy, hidey, barnyard fermented*, *musty*, and *Rioy* (strongly medicinal; so named after the inexpensive, strip-picked coffees often shipped through the Brazilian port of Rio de Janeiro).

ESPRESSO TASTING TERMS

The following terms often come up informally in discussions of espresso coffees, though more as terms of connoisseurship than of trade. They relate as much to the effects of brewing and roasting as to the qualities of the original green bean and are less clearly defined than the technical tasting terms described earlier.

Sweet. Particularly in Italy, where espresso is most often drunk without milk, the *sweetness* of an espresso coffee is important. The sweetness this term describes is not a literal sugariness, but rather a sensation of richness, smoothness, and heaviness in the cup, probably related to suspended colloids in the brewed coffee. Sweetness in an espresso blend is related to *heavy body*, *low acidity*, and *balanced flavor* in the beans, a dark-brown but not black style in the roast, and proper brewing technique.

Bitter. The *bitter* bite of some espresso coffees and blends should be distinguished from the acidy tones of a medium-roast coffee, since the bitterness described here is a taste characteristic created by dark-roasting. It is not necessarily an unpleasant characteristic; most West Coast American and many Latin American and southern Italian blends are rather bitter by design. Espresso drinkers in those regions find the lighter-roasted blends preferred by northern Italians bland by comparison. If the distinction between bitter and acidy seems abstract, an analogy might help: Acidity is like the "dry" sensation in most wines, a mild astringent sensation toward the back of the palate. The bitter sensation that arises from dark-roasting is more analogous to the bitterness of certain aperitifs like Campari, for example; it is a more total and dominating sensation, and less localized on the palate.

Smooth. I take *smooth* to be an epithet describing an espresso coffee that can be taken comfortably without milk and with very little sugar; a coffee in which a heavy body and the sweet sensation described above predominate over bitter and acidy tones.

Bittersweet. This is my term for the positive flavor complex developed by dark-roasting. In my experience that complex combines the heavy body and smooth richness described above as *sweet* with the sensation described above as *bitter*. What I call the *bittersweetness* of dark-roasted coffees is a taste taken for granted by professionals and experienced coffee aficionados but a cause of misunderstanding in communications between coffee sellers and novice consumers. The average North American filter coffee drinker will call the taste that I call bittersweet *strong*, to my mind an inappropriate term. For example, a wildly acidy coffee like Ethiopian Harrar brought to a light or medium roast is every bit as "strong" tasting as any dark-roasted coffee. *Strong* properly refers to the amount of solids and other flavoring agents in the brewed coffee. A dark-roasted coffee could be brewed *strong*, as it is in the espresso method, or *weak*, as it might be in a filter-drip system when one is stingy with the ground coffee.

WHAT MAKES GREEN BEANS DIFFERENT

If green coffee beans do embody differing taste characteristics, what causes these differences? The following pages describe factors influencing coffee quality and flavor in the green bean before it has been subjected to subsequent processes like blending, roasting, decaffeination, and brewing. They include botanical species and variety; growing altitude and conditions; processing; certain intangibles of soil, climate, and location; and age, or the length of time the bean has been held between processing and roasting. The final pages of this section describe how these factors are used by traders to divide the world's coffee production into three broad commercial categories: robustas, Brazils, and milds.

Botany

Species. All of the world's finest coffees, and some that are not so fine, belong to the species *Coffea arabica*, the species that first hooked the world on coffee. Second in importance among coffee species is *Coffea robusta*, a lower-growing, more disease-resistant, heavier-bearing species of the coffee tree. *C. robusta* produces a bean that is rounder in shape than the arabica bean, blander in flavor, somewhat heavier in caffeine content, and cheaper than most arabica. Coffee from the robusta species has little importance in the world of fancy medium-roast coffee but figures prominently in discussions of espresso blends. Other species, such as *Coffea liberica* and *Coffea arabusta*, the latter a hybrid developed by the Ivory Coast government combining qualities of both arabica and robusta, are not now commercially important in the larger picture, although they may at some point become so.

Variety. Botanical variety also has an effect on the quality and cup characteristics of coffee. Earlier varieties of *C. arabica* were spontaneous developments; they include the famous and widely distributed *var. bourbon*, which evolved on the Island of Réunion in the Indian Ocean in the eighteenth century; *var. old chick* (for "old Chikmagalgur"), a variety of Arabica that evolved from the earliest trees planted in India by the pilgrim Baba Budans in the seventeenth century; and the odd and rapidly disappearing *var. maragogipe* (Mah-rah-go-ZHEE-pay), which produces a very large, porous bean and first appeared in Maragogipe, Brazil.

Coffees from such traditional varieties—often collectively referred to as *old arabicas*—are particularly valued in the fancy coffee world. They may be a disappearing delicacy, however. Recently, green revolution scientists working in the growing countries have produced varieties of arabica that are more disease-resistant, heavier-bearing, and faster to reach maturity than the older, traditional

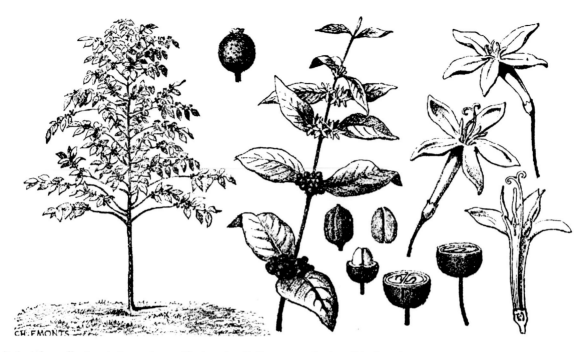

At the left a coffee tree; in the center a coffee branch, with flowers near the top of the branch modulating to ripe fruit near the bottom. At right are representations of the coffee flower, which is white in color, and below that illustrations demonstrating the relationship of the coffee seed or bean to the coffee fruit.

varieties. *Var. coturra*, developed in Colombia and now widely planted there, is an example. Most fancy coffee dealers consider coffee produced by these newer varieties inferior to beans produced by the old arabica varieties. I would agree.

Altitude

The *C. arabica* species grows at altitudes ranging from around 1,500 to 6,000 feet. Generally, the higher grown the coffee the more slowly the seed, or bean, develops, and the harder and denser the bean. Such *high-grown* or *hard-bean* coffees are valued in the world market because in general they display a heavier body, a more complex flavor, and a more pronounced and vibrant acidity than lower-grown coffees. Some celebrated coffees from other parts of the world are cultivated at intermediate altitudes, however, including the best Hawaiian and Sumatran coffees. The inexpensive, mass-processed arabica coffees of Brazil are grown at an altitude of about 2,000 feet; robusta coffees typically grow at even lower elevations.

Processing

The care with which coffee is picked, the manner in which the fruit is removed from the bean, and the way in which the bean is dried after removal of the fruit all profoundly affect coffee taste and quality.

Picking. Coffee fruit does not ripen uniformly. Both ripe and unripe berries, or "cherries" as they are called in the coffee trade, festoon the same branch. The best coffees are hand-picked as they ripen. Cheaper coffees are stripped from the trees in a single operation, thus combining ripe, unripe, and overripe berries, not to mention leaves, twigs, and dirt, in the same batch.

Removing the Fruit From the Bean. Common wisdom in the coffee trade declares that *wet processing*, in which the outer layers of the coffee fruit are carefully removed from the seed or bean in a complex set of operations *before* the bean is dried, produces the best coffee. The same wisdom declares that *dry-processed* or *natural* coffee, in which the fruit and skin are allowed to shrivel and dry around the bean, then later removed by abrasion, is inferior to such *wet-processed* or *washed* coffee. Generally, this distinction holds, but many of the world's best and most interesting coffees are either dry-processed (Yemen Mocha), or processed in a way that combines wet- and dry-processing (most Sumatran coffees).

What really counts is the *care* taken in processing the coffee, regardless of method. Most dry-processed coffees are also strip-picked and carelessly handled, which means that overripe, rotting fruit and other vegetable matter (not to mention whatever animal matter happens to be on the ground at the time) are piled together during the drying process, tainting the flavor of the entire batch. Such practices have given dry-processing an undeservedly bad reputation.

In fact, coffee that has been dry-processed with care often displays a more complex flavor than the more predictable taste of wet-processed coffee, probably owing to the effect of the fruit drying around the bean. Dry-processed coffees often exhibit a subtle earthy or wild flavor, for example, which many coffee fanciers value.

Cleaning and Sorting the Beans. In general, the more care taken in removing various unwanted material—stones, twigs, discolored or immature beans, and the like—from the sound coffee beans, the cleaner and fuller the flavor of the coffee will be and the higher price it will command. The cleaning and sorting process can be done by machine, by hand, or by some combination of both. *European preparation* describes coffee that has been prepared, cleaned, and sorted carefully enough to look good in whole-bean form after roasting. At one time Europeans sold their coffees primarily in whole bean form, whereas North Americans sold theirs primarily pre-ground and packaged; hence "European preparation."

Grading. Grading is a process that assigns value to coffees for purposes of trading. It ultimately is a kind of sophisticated sorting that divides a given country's coffee production into categories according to various quality-related criteria. These criteria vary from country to country but typically include number of defects (defects include everything from broken or misshapen beans to sticks), size of the bean (bigger is usually better), growing

(continued on page 77)

Organic and Other Chemical-Free Coffees

Organic coffees are coffees whose growing conditions and processing have been certified by one of several independent monitoring and testing agencies to be free of the use of pesticides, herbicides, and other potentially harmful chemicals. The agency conducts inspections of the farms and processing facilities, tests the soil and plants, and generally monitors the progress of the coffee from tree to marketplace. This process is understandably costly.

Alternatives to Organic

If organic coffees existed only to protect the consumer from potentially harmful agricultural residues, there would be (and are) simpler and cheaper ways to meet the same need. Consumers could simply buy a traditional coffee grown naturally, like Yemen Mocha or Ethiopian Harrar. Or they could buy a coffee that has been subjected to independent laboratory tests to verify that it does not contain harmful chemical residues. Such coffees are now appearing in specialty stores. Or they could simply forget about the whole issue and drink whatever coffee came along. Since we consume only the seed of the coffee fruit, not the fruit itself, and since we subject that seed to roasting and steeping, and subsquently consume only the water that the roasted seed has been steeped in, it is highly unlikely that even the slightest traces of chemicals that might have been used in growing the original fruit reach the cup or our stomachs.

More Vehicle than End in Itself

But consumers who buy a certified organic coffee are often supporting a complex set of goals and processes in which the consumer health issue is more vehicle than end in itself. Although some of the certified organic coffees emerging on the market today come from small farms or estates, many are produced by small peasant growers who have been assisted in organizing themselves into cooperatives that share processing facilities, agricultural information, and various forms of mutual assistance. Although such cooperatives are common wherever coffee is grown on small plots, the cooperatives that grow organic coffees stress the well-established procedures of organic farming: composting, organic pest control, etc.

In return, the farmers obtain a premium for their coffee. Because the coffee they grow is certified organic, they have an opportunity to bypass the usual export channels and to move their coffee into the consuming country via businesspeople who specialize in fine coffee or organic produce. Thus, farmers who a few years before might have been selling their coffee to people cruising the backroads in trucks, buying coffee at pennies a pound, now may be selling it through a cooperative to specialists in organic produce or fine coffees. The process is facilitated by a loose network of those who promote organic agriculture in the growing countries and those importers and roasters who promote organic produce in the consuming countries.

Organic certification is the key to the success of the entire process. Its cost and the cost of the somewhat lower yields occasioned by the organic method are passed on to the consumer, who pays a little more for a guaranteed pure product, in the process supporting more sustainable agricultural practices and a better life for a number of small coffee growers.

Organic Coffee and Espresso

The cup quality of organic coffees is the subject of debate among specialty coffee professionals, with skeptics claiming that most organic beans appearing in their cupping rooms are overpriced and under-flavored, and believers citing the latest splendid organic coffees that they tasted just yesterday.

Two points are certain. First, despite what the skeptics say, there are many excellent organic coffees now available. Second, those who confine themselves only to organic coffees are severely limiting their range of coffee experience. At this writing the organic concept appears to have established itself in only select regions of the coffee-growing world. The many wonderful coffees from other parts of the world arrive on North American shores as they always have, somewhat mysteriously, with little documentation on the details of their processing and cultivation.

On the other hand, espresso aficionados are in a better position in regard to organic coffees than their medium-roast-drinking colleagues, since the organic concept is particularly well established in southern Mexico and in Peru, two areas producing coffees that make particularly sweet, smooth dark-roasts. Still, even with dark roasts, one's coffee adventures will be limited if one sticks to organic beans alone.

It seems inevitable that the organic market niche will grow and with it will come more coffees, and better coffees. In the meantime, there doubtless will be many people who will choose to drink slightly more expensive coffee with slightly fewer choices in order to support the goals and aspirations of the organic coffee movement, while assuring themselves of an absolutely pure product.

altitude (higher is usually better), method of processing (wet vs. dry), and cup quality.

Age of the Beans

Coffees that are roasted and sold soon after processing are called *new crop* and generally display more acidity, brighter, clearer flavor notes, and a thinner body than *old crop* coffees, which have been held in warehouses for a year or two before roasting; *mature* coffees, which have been held for two to three years; or *vintage* or *aged* coffees, which have been held for several years. The longer coffees are held, the heavier their body and the more muted their acidity becomes, until, in aged or vintage coffees, the acidity and other subtle aromatics disappear altogether to be replaced by a rather static heaviness. I would not call aged coffees rich; rather they are simply heavy, almost syrupy. Aged coffees are sometimes used in premium espresso blends to balance younger, brighter coffees.

Monsooned Malabar is a special kind of older coffee produced in India by exposing dry-processed arabica coffees to monsoon winds in open warehouses. The ambient moisture seems to partly replace the original moisture in the bean, producing a variant on the thick, rather toneless taste typical of older coffees.

Soil, Climate, and Other Geographic Intangibles

Certain coffees are world-famous: Jamaican Blue Mountain, for example, and Yemen Mocha. Others should be, such as Ethiopian Yirgacheffe and the best Sumatran and Kenyan coffees. Such coffees, which are grown in certain limited geographical areas, all have certain distinct flavor characteristics that coffee fanciers admire. Yirgacheffe is gentle, flowery, and fruity, for example; Yemen Mocha has a gamey, wild twist to its acidity. The best Kenyan AA has a full, bell-like, overpowering acidity alive with fruity, wine-like notes, while the best Sumatran coffees are extraordinarily rich and full in the mouth, with a long finish and a low-toned, subtle acidity. The true Wallensford Estate Blue Mountain, which hardly can be found anymore and when it is may be disappointing, was at its best a subtle, balanced coffee, extraordinary for its completeness.

These flavor characteristics are undoubtedly owing to a combination of factors: botanical species and variety, altitude, method of picking and processing, and local climate and soil.

The rarest and most expensive of the world's coffees are not used in espresso blends. Dark-roasting mutes most of the qualities that make these coffees distinctive, and to incorporate them into a blend would be to waste the very qualities that make them valuable. Other coffees that are just as distinctive but less expensive are often used in dark-roast blends, however. These include Kenyan AA and Indonesian coffees like Sumatran. Kenyan is often added to espresso blends because it is a strong, bold coffee that holds its own in a blend and because it is relatively inexpensive, consistent, and widely available. Sumatran, moderately priced given its quality, and also widely available, makes a pleasantly low-key espresso on its own, and adds rich undertones and body to an espresso blend.

GLOBAL COFFEE CATEGORIES

To provide a starting point for trading, coffee merchants often divide the coffees of the world into three broad market categories based on some of the factors described in the preceding pages. These categories are worth noting, since they figure prominently in discussions of blending for espresso cuisine.

Milds. This category includes all of the best coffees of the *C. arabica* species, ranging from the rarest to those decent-quality but relatively undistinguished growths used as the basis for most North American espresso blends. The numerous origins and qualities of coffee in this category are collectively called milds to distinguish them from the harsher-tasting, strip-picked and mass-processed arabica coffees in the *Brazils* category.

Brazils. In the coffee world *Brazils* describes arabica coffees grown on large Brazilian plantations and usually strip-picked and relatively carelessly processed and sorted. This category is sometimes extended to include all dry-processed arabicas of lesser quality, regardless of where they are grown. The best Brazilian coffees, which have been picked and processed with care, are categorized with the *milds* described above.

Robustas. The *robustas* category includes all coffees from the *C. robusta* species. They generally constitute the bargain coffees of the world, although some of the best and most carefully processed may compete in price with the Brazils and lesser milds.

BLENDS AND BLENDING

Blends can combine coffees brought to different degrees of roast, coffees with different caffeine contents, and/or straight coffees from different origins.

For example, roasters frequently blend darker and lighter roasts to produce a more complex flavor than can be obtained with coffees brought to the same roast. Blending also is used to modulate caffeine content; caffeine-free and ordinary beans are often combined in varying proportions to produce blends with half the caffeine in ordinary coffee, or two thirds, or one third, etc.

Much more common, however, and more challenging, is blending coffees of approximately the same caffeine content and roast. As practiced in the commercial coffee business, such blending has complex goals. The commercial blender aspires to cut costs while keeping quality high and wants to assemble a blend with consistent taste even though the straight coffees that make up the blend may change. Certain coffees are not always available; some coffees may be cheaper than others at certain times of the year, and so on. But the blend has to taste more or less the same every time, or the customers will be disappointed. So commercial blenders may find themselves amid a shifting kaleidoscope of prices and availabilities, constantly juggling coffees in an attempt to keep the taste the same and the cost down.

For specialty roasters the goal is a bit simpler. A few larger specialty roasters, like their commercial counterparts, may blend for price but with less urgency and compromise. The overriding goal of specialty store blenders is simply producing a coffee that is more complete and pleasing in its totality than any of its unblended components would be alone.

Complete and Pleasing?

In the case of an espresso blend, what constitutes "more complete and pleasing" is obviously relative: relative to the palate of the blender, to the expectations of the consumer, and to the traditions to which both blender and consumer refer.

At this point it might be useful to refer to the array of tasting terms listed earlier: acidity, body, aroma, finish, sweetness, bitterness, and so on.

It would be safe to say that all espresso blends everywhere aspire to as full a body as possible, as much sweet sensation as possible, and as much aroma and as long and resonant a finish as possible.

The differences arise with acidity and with the bitter side of the bittersweet taste equation. Most northern Italian roasters present blends with almost no acidy notes whatsoever, whereas North American espresso blends tend to maintain the dry, acidy undertones most Americans and Canadians are accustomed to in their lighter-roasted coffees. This difference is simply a matter of choice and tradition. North Americans are used to acidy, high-grown Latin American coffees, and Italians are accustomed to drinking either African robustas or lower-altitude Brazilian arabicas.

My own position, for what it's worth, is that acidy notes need to be felt but not tasted in espresso blends. They should be barely discernible, yet vibrating slightly in the heart of the blend.

Recall that acidity, or dryness, is a property of the bean that diminishes as the roast becomes darker, to eventually be replaced entirely by the bittersweet, pungent flavor notes characteristic of dark roasts. The value of the bitter side of the bittersweet equation is also an issue in blending philosophy, with northern Italian roasters coming down more on the bitter*sweet* side, and southern Italian and North American roasters leaning more toward the *bitter*sweet. As I pointed out in discussing style of roast, this difference is reflected in the somewhat lighter roasts preferred by northern Italian roasters, opposed to the darker styles favored by most North American and southern Italian roasters.

So on both accounts, blending philosophy and style of roast, northern Italians put a premium on sweetness and smoothness and North Americans and southern Italians on punch.

It is clear why North Americans might prefer a punchier, more pungent and more acidy espresso coffee; they need the power of such flavor notes to carry through all of the milk they tend to add to their "lattes," cappuccinos, etc. Italians generally take their espresso undiluted and so might logically prefer a smoother, sweeter blend. But such an explanation may be entirely too rational; after all, those purist Italians also tend to dump large quantities of sugar into their smooth, sweet espresso blends. Probably taste in espresso blends is simply another irrationality of culture and tradition.

Achieving Blending Goals

At any rate, if heavy body, seductive aroma, a slight acidity, and a rich bittersweetness are the goals, how does one attempt to achieve these goals in blending?

Milds, Brazils, and Robustas. For an answer, we need to first return to the three broad market categories for green coffees described earlier in this chapter: milds, Brazils, and robustas. The *milds* category, you may recall, includes all of the better coffees of the world of the *C. arabica* species. The *Brazils* category includes the cheaper, strip-picked and dry-processed arabicas from the plantations of south-central Brazil, and *robustas* all coffees of the species *C. robusta*.

For the espresso blender, setting aside the question of price (obviously most robustas win the day on that score) each of these three categories has something to contribute to a blend, as well as some drawbacks.

The best mild coffees have substantial body and acidity. For the espresso blender, body is always desirable, not only for itself but because it contributes to the sensation of "sweetness" in a dark roast. The acidy notes are more problematic, however. The sharpness they contribute to a blend may be desirable for North American tastes and for blends intended to be used in drinks involving hot frothed milk, but they are less desirable in blends intended for those who drink their espresso without milk and prefer a sweet, smooth cup in the classic northern Italian style. Finally, a blend made up only of very acidy coffees, like Kenyan, for example, will not make the best dark roast by almost anyone's standards.

The middle-category Brazils, or cheap, dry-processed arabicas, make a reasonable basis for an espresso blend, providing that they are not off-tasting or "Rioy." These coffees tend to be mildly acidy and decent in body, and probably figure in many Italian espresso blends. North American specialty roasters, perhaps because of their background in the fancy, or specialty, coffee trade, usually substitute a lesser quality mild coffee for the Brazils in their dark-roast blends.

Finally, the robustas. As I indicated earlier, robustas tend to be bland and lacking in acidity, complex flavor notes, and aroma. The better robustas have a full body that seems to develop particularly well in a dark roast, however. Most Italian roasters add some robustas to their espresso blends, sometimes as much as 80 percent or more; probably only the premium Italian blends incorporate no robustas whatsoever. Italian-American roasters tend to join their North American colleagues in avoiding the use of large percentages of robustas, but some, particularly those who maintain close ties with Italian practice, may add small quantities of high-quality robustas to their espresso blends.

Those Italians who use robustas often argue that they produce more crema, the golden froth that covers the surface of a good demitasse of espresso. I find no evidence that robustas produce more crema, although they do produce a darker crema. In fact, robustas are probably favored by many Italian roasters because they are less expensive than the better arabicas, because they mellow sharper coffees in a blend, producing a smoother and more palatable cup of straight espresso, and because of tradition: The Italian African colonies of the early half of the twentieth century produced mainly robusta coffees, and Italian coffee drinkers became accustomed to the sweeter, flatter taste of robustas in their espresso.

Robustas in North American Espresso. Most North American specialty roasters absolutely eschew robustas, however, and generally consider them something just short of poison. A coffee broker who caters to specialty roasters recently told me that he was afraid to even handle robustas, for fear that he might acquire a reputation for tolerating poor-quality coffees. Such fears may seem paranoid to an outsider, but the specialty coffee business operates a good deal on trust and reputation, and roasters who approve a sample of a high-quality, expensive coffee want to feel certain that the high-quality coffee they ordered actually will be delivered, without clandestine adulteration by cheaper or inferior beans.

North American specialty roasters' negative view of robustas has been strengthened over the years by the dubious practices of commercial coffee concerns, who have betrayed the continent's long-established love affair with coffee by using increasing quantities of bland, lifeless robustas in low-cost commercial instant and canned blends. Thus robustas justifiably have assumed the role of bad guy in the great morality play of the selling out of the North American coffee drinker.

A second reason North American fancy coffee roasters avoid robustas relates to the history of the specialty coffee trade. Since most of their business until recently was in fancy, unblended arabica coffees, many North American specialty roasters are only now learning how to fine-tune their espresso blends. The tendency until recently was simply to dark-roast whatever one had too much of or could get a good price on, which generally meant decent-quality mild coffees, because decent-quality milds were the only "price" coffees in the warehouse of a self-respecting specialty roaster.

Today, however, with the growing interest in sophisticated espresso blends, good robustas used in small quantities for their positive cup qualities, rather than for their low price, probably have a future in North American specialty espresso roasting.

CHOOSING THE COFFEE

Espresso Break

Coffee Speak: The Specialty Coffee Lexicon

Choosing a coffee for home espresso brewing ought to be an ongoing adventure. Although the subtler distinctions among unblended varietal coffees are lost in dark-roasting, the rich diversity of styles of roast, dark-roast blends, and varietal coffees becoming available in North American markets presents the espresso drinker with a gratifying arena for experiment and connoisseurship.

CANS, BAGS, AND BULK

Coffee suitable for espresso brewing can be purchased in three forms: pre-ground in cans; whole bean in cans and bags; and whole bean in bulk. Both blended and unblended coffees are available in all three forms, although buying whole beans in bulk offers the espresso drinker by far the greatest number of blends and straight coffees to choose from.

For the true aficionado, there also is the alternative of buying coffee green and roasting it at home. Home roasters can assemble a veritable cellar of fine coffees, since in its green state coffee keeps very well. Enough instruction to get started roasting at home is given on pages 55–58.

Commercial vs. Specialty Coffees

Pre-ground coffee sold in cans and bags is often called *commercial* coffee, and whole-bean coffees, either packaged or in bulk, *specialty* or *fancy* coffee. Commercial coffee is usually roasted in large plants controlled by general food companies, and distributed regionally or nationally, whereas specialty or fancy coffees generally are roasted in smaller-scale facilities by privately held firms strongly marked by the personality of their owners, and sold locally. Commercial coffees are part of the larger, conventionally organized world of food production and distribution, whereas specialty coffees have created a relatively distinct culture of specialized producers and dedicated consumers who share a common ground of coffee connoisseurship.

Canned Pre-Ground Blends

Commercial canned pre-ground coffees are almost always blends; the only exception I'm aware of at this writing is a dark-roast Colombian. Many of the most widely distributed canned dark-roast coffees are ground far too coarsely for home espresso brewing. If you are a novice trying home espresso brewing for the first time, do *not* start with a canned dark-roast coffee ground for all-purpose brewing. The coarse grind will only lead to watery, under-extracted coffee and frustration. Several packaged dark-roast coffees *are* ground to espresso specifications, however. The labels of these true espresso coffees usually carry language on the can like "ground extra-fine for espresso brewing."

Espresso "pods" (see pages 117) are a variation on canned pre-ground coffees. Pods are tea-bag-like, single-serving-sized paper sacks of ground, blended espresso intended to fit into proprietary filters provided with certain pump espresso machines. I see little advantage to pods over a good canned espresso blend, but they may be reassuring to the beginner, since they guarantee a proper dose of ground coffee.

In style, canned dark-roast blends range from mild, sweet blends prepared in northern Italy to reflect classic Italian taste, to much more darkly roasted coffees with an earthy twist intended for "the Latin taste," as the language on the can usually puts it, to a 100 percent Colombian with dry, acidy notes vibrating inside the bittersweetness of the dark-roast flavor. These canned pre-ground coffees can provide a helpful orientation to the range of experience possible in espresso-style blends.

Nevertheless, canned commercial coffees are limited in several respects. First of all, canned coffees simply cannot deliver a cup of espresso as fresh as can recently roasted whole-bean coffees ground immediately before brewing. Second, canned coffees do not offer the espresso aficionado the variety that whole-bean coffees do.

Buying Whole-Bean Coffees for Espresso

Whole-bean coffees sold in bags at supermarkets can be excellent, but expiration dates are never printed on the bags, and the buyer has no idea whatsoever how long these packages have sat on the shelf, wooing passersby with their wine label prose and elegant logos. By far the best place to buy whole-bean coffee for espresso brewing is in bulk at a specialty coffee store or counter with a large volume and a knowledgeable management. If the store actually roasts its coffees on the premises, so much the better. Locations of such stores can usually be found in the telephone classified pages under the "retail coffee" heading.

Those isolated from centers where specialty coffees are sold or those who find it inconvenient to shop for coffee regularly may find ordering bulk coffee by mail useful. Readers who have trouble identifying a source may wish to consult the resource guide in the companion volume to this one, *Coffee: A Guide to Buying, Brewing, and Enjoying*. Coffees should be ordered through the mails only in whole-bean form; unprotected ground coffees are likely to be half-staled by the time they land on the porch. This means that a good grinder is needed to enjoy mail-order coffee; consult Chapter 7 for details on espresso grinding and grinders.

SPECIALTY STORE DECISIONS

The range of choice one faces upon entering a specialty coffee store can be daunting. The reader may wish to skim through the Espresso Break on Coffee Speak on pages 88–91 for an orientation to specialty coffee terminology. Some coffee choices exceed the scope of this chapter: selecting among caffeine-free coffees treated by various competing decaffeination processes, for example, or choosing between organically grown coffees and conventionally grown coffees. Some help is offered for these decisions in the Espresso Breaks on Coffee Speak (pages 88–91), Decaffeination Processes (pages 63–68), and Organic Coffees (pages 74–76).

But once such health-related concerns have been responded to, the subtler and perhaps more interesting decisions remain: what style of roast to buy; whether to buy a blended or unblended dark-roast coffee; which

Weighing bulk beans at a specialty coffee store, coffee bins in the background.

blended or unblended dark-roast coffee to buy; and finally, whether and how to assemble blends of one's own.

CHOOSING A ROAST

As indicated earlier, any style of roast can be prepared in an espresso machine and used to assemble espresso drinks, but only a dark brown roast, darker than the typical North American roast but not black, will produce the flavor we associate with espresso. See pages 50 and 53 for a discussion of the various roasts, page 52 for a descriptive chart of roasts and their names, and Chapter 4 for more on the process and philosophy of roasting.

Roasts range in style from those that are only somewhat darker than the American norm (often called *Viennese* or *Light French*), with only slight traces of oil on the surface of the bean, to an almost black preparation with an extremely oily surface (*Dark French, Neapolitan*, etc.). The classic espresso roast (*Italian, Espresso, French*) is somewhere between, dark brown with a moderately oily surface. Coffees roasted toward the lighter end of the espresso spectrum retain some of the brisk, acidy tones characteristic of medium-roasted coffees; coffees roasted near the middle of the spectrum lose almost all acidy notes, replacing them with the bittersweet flavor complex typical of darker-roast coffees; the very darkest roasts begin to lose body and display the slightly charred flavor typical of these nearly black styles.

Coffees brought to a dark roast slowly, at relatively low temperatures, may display a peculiar pungent, almost sour flavor twist. It is not an unpleasant taste but takes getting used to. In North America this flavor turns up in certain canned dark-roast blends intended for the Latin taste.

The Complex Relationship of Roast and Blend

Choosing espresso coffee by roast is complicated by the fact that most coffees intended for the espresso cuisine are blends, and the composition of the blend may either offset or reinforce taste tendencies created by style of roast. Generally, those roasters who prefer a mild, sweet espresso will pursue their objective on two fronts. They will use coffees with low acidity in their blends and will also bring that blend of low-acidity coffees to a relatively light espresso roast to avoid the bitter notes characteristic of darker roasts. On the other hand, those who prefer sharpness and punch in their espresso blends may use highly acidy coffees *and* bring those acidy blends to a relatively dark roast, thus emphasizing both acidity and the bitter side of the bittersweet dark-roast flavor equation. The effect of roast on coffee flavor can be fully understood only by roasting coffee at home, or by finding a roaster who offers the same straight or unblended coffees in a variety of styles of roast.

BLENDED VS. UNBLENDED COFFEES IN ESPRESSO

Most of those who qualify as espresso experts argue for the superiority of blended espresso coffees over unblended. Their arguments often appear self-serving, however, since most experts are also in the business of selling coffee, and blends have several advantages for the coffee seller. First, they enable the seller to develop in customers a loyalty to a certain blend, rather than loyalty to a more generic unblended varietal; second, they promote a mystification of the blending and roasting process, both of which are somewhat simpler than roasters make them out to be; and third, blends enable the more cost-conscious roaster to cut costs while maintaining quality.

Given all of that, good blends doubtless do produce a more satisfying espresso over the long haul, at least for those who prefer consistency over experiment and surprise. But for those who enjoy variety, unblended dark-roasted coffees and the opportunity they afford for creating one's own blends offer a pleasant opportunity for connoisseurship.

Espresso blends and blending are discussed in detail near the end of Chapter 5. Once the issues and principles of espresso blending are understood, the next step is actually tasting a variety of blends. In the San Francisco

(continued on page 92)

COFFEE SPEAK: THE SPECIALTY COFFEE LEXICON

Variety, one of the attractions of the specialty coffee store, can also be one of its frustrations. Most stores carry at least 20 different coffees; some may carry as many as 50. The sheer babble of names and the repetitive shades of brown in the bins can intimidate and confuse. Here are a few rules of thumb to assist in making sense of specialty coffee cacophony.

European Names Usually Describe Blends of Dark Roast Coffee. *Viennese, Italian, French, Neapolitan, Spanish,* and *European* are all frequently used names for generic blends of coffee roasted darker than the (usually unnamed) American roast. Espresso and Continental are also popular names for generic dark roast blends. Most coffees described by these terms are roasted in a style suitable for espresso cuisine; choosing from among them is a matter of taste. See the Espresso Break on pages 51–52 for a complete list of roast names, and Chapter 4 for more on roasting and styles of roast.

Non-European Names Usually Describe Unblended or Straight Coffees. Coffees sold in straight or unblended form, also called *varietal coffees,* typically carry the name of the country in which they were grown: *Kenyan, Colombian, Costa Rican,* etc. If these coffees have been brought to a darker roast suitable for the espresso cuisine, they will usually carry a double-decker name: *Dark-Roast Kenyan, Colombian Dark Roast,* etc. For some advice on choosing among unblended dark-roast coffees see Chapter 6.

Most unblended or varietal coffees also carry a subordinate set of names intended to narrow the growing geography a bit and spice up the sales pitch on signs and brochures. These names usually represent market names, of which there are thousands in the coffee trade; or grade names, which are only a bit less numerous and confusing than market names; or estate names, which are the names of the farms where the coffees have been grown and processed.

Market names usually refer to the region or district in which the coffee is grown (Mexican *Coatepec*), the main market town or village in that region (Guatemala *Antigua*), the port through which the coffee is shipped (Brazilian *Santos*), or none of the above, which means that the original geographical source of the name has been lost in the mists of time and preserved principally on the burlap of coffee sacks and in the jargon of coffee traders.

Grade names usually refer to the altitude at which the coffee is grown (particularly in central America); to the size of the bean; to numbers of defects (discolored beans, sticks, pebbles, etc.); to the nature of the processing (wet-processing vs. dry-processing); or to cup quality, or how clean and characteristic of the region the coffee tastes.

Altitude is reflected in grading terms like *high grown*, *hard bean* (the higher the growing altitude the denser and harder the bean), and *altura* (Spanish for "height" or "summit"). Grade names keyed to bean size usually are alphabetical (*A* is the highest grade in India; *AA* the highest in Kenya, Tanzania and New Guinea; *AAA* in Peru). Wet-processed coffees tend to be differentiated from dry-processed coffees by relatively self-evident terms like *washed* and the Spanish term for washed, *lavado*. Finally, some grading systems may simply employ a hierarchy of superlatives (in Colombia *supremo* is the best grade, *extra* is second-best, and *excelso* a grade combining beans from both).

To summarize, one may see names that look like the following: *Kenyan AA Dark Roast* (a high-grade Kenyan coffee brought to a dark roast suitable for espresso cuisine); *French Roast Altura Coatepec* (a high-grown coffee from the Mexican region of Coatepec brought to an extremely dark roast); *Espresso Roast Sumatran Lintong* (a Sumatran coffee that bears the market name Lintong and has been brought to a roast suitable for espresso); and so on.

For more on names of varietal coffees and discussion of their cup characteristics see the companion volume to this book, *Coffee: A Guide to Buying, Brewing, and Enjoying*.

Fanciful, Whimsical, Advertising Romantic, and People Names Usually Describe House Blends. In an effort to establish brand loyalty and develop a sort of store mystique most specialty roasters offer house blends, usually mysteriously named and effusively, if vaguely, described. ("An exotic blend of robust Indonesian, pungent East African, and brisk Central American growths, carefully proportioned and roasted to bring out the full power and bouquet of these rare and exotic origins. Named after the roastmaster's favorite niece.") These blends are usually excellent and worth experimenting with; one only wishes the copy writers patronized less and communicated more. Many of these proprietary blends are dark-roast and intended for espresso cuisine.

Names that Sound Like Cocktails or Candy Describe Flavored Coffees. Flavored coffees are decent-quality arabica coffees brought to a medium roast, then coated with various flavoring agents. The flavorings are variations of those used in countless other foods. Sometimes nut fragments are added to the flavored beans to dress them up. The names for flavored coffees (*Pina Colada, Vanilla Nut, Frangelica Cream*) attempt to evoke associations with pleasurable experiences like vacations and dessert, and usually are as carefully contrived as the flavorings themselves. Many specialty roasters refuse to have flavored coffees in their stores; others carry them with varying degrees of enthusiasm.

Since most flavored coffees are brought to a medium roast, they do not figure prominently in espresso cuisine. Some espresso drinkers like to add small quantities of flavored beans to their espresso blends before grinding.

Names for Decaffeination Processes and Organic Growing Practices Are Stacked on Top of Everything Else. Still another layer of coffee naming has been created by decaffeination processes and organic or chemical-free growing practices.

Decaffeinated or caffeine-free coffees have had the caffeine soaked out of them; they are delivered to the roaster green, like any other coffee. Roasters in most metropolitan centers offer a variety of coffees in decaffeinated form. The origin of the beans and style of roast usually are still designated: *Caffeine-Free French Roast Colombian*, for instance, or *Decaffeinated Dark-Roast Special House Blend*, etc.

Three general processes are currently used to decaffeinate specialty coffees. The names applied to them are occasionally misleading. In the *water-only, Swiss-Water,* or *French-Water* process, the green beans are soaked in hot water, from which the caffeine is removed by means of activated charcoal filters. *Conventional process, traditional process,* or *European process* all refer to methods in which the caffeine has been removed from the hot water (*not* from the beans themselves) by means of a solvent, rather than by charcoal filters. Solvents currently in use are methylene chloride and ethyl acetate. Ethyl acetate occurs naturally in fruit, so coffees decaffeinated by processes making use of it are sometimes called *natural process decaffeinated*. Finally, coffees are beginning to appear that have been decaffeinated by direct treatment of the bean with a combination of water and compressed, semiliquid form of carbon dioxide (CO_2). These coffees are usually marketed as CO_2 *Process* or *Sparkling Water*

Process decaffeinated (the latter an allusion to the two ingredients of sparkling water, CO_2 and water). For more on decaffeination processes, see pages 63–68.

Properly defined, *organic coffees* are those coffees certified by various international monitoring agencies as having been grown without the use of agricultural chemicals. Some retailers may call a coffee *organic* because laboratory tests have shown it to be free of residues of harmful agricultural chemicals, but such coffees should be called *chemical-free* rather than *organic*. Organic connotes an entire agricultural and environmental program, not simply a product that tests have shown to be free of chemical residues. For more on organic coffees, see the Espresso Break on pages 74–76.

Organic is a qualifier added to all the rest of the qualifying adjectives possible to pile onto a specialty coffee. So, if you're ready for this, it might be possible to see a coffee in a specialty store named, for example, *Dark Roast Swiss-Water–Process Decaffeinated Organic Mexican Chiapas*, or a Mexican coffee from the state of Chiapas that has been grown and processed without the use of chemicals, has been treated to remove the caffeine by use of hot water and charcoal filtering, and has been brought to a dark roast suitable for espresso cuisine.

Since specialty coffee roasters justifiably question the viability of their customers' attention span when confronted with such breathless nomenclature, multiple qualifying terms are usually dispersed in the signage system, relegated to the fine print, or condensed by leaving something out.

Some Terms Don't Fit into any Category. Here are a last few terms that defy easy categorization: *Turkish coffee* refers to neither coffee from Turkey nor style of roast. The name designates grind of coffee and style of brewing. *Turkish* is a common name for a medium- to dark-roast coffee, ground to a powder, sweetened, boiled, and served with the sediment still in the cup. As indicated earlier, *Viennese* usually describes a somewhat darker-than-normal style of roast, but it also can describe a blend of roasts (about half dark and half medium), or, in Great Britain, a blend of coffee and roast fig. *New Orleans coffee* is either a dark-roast coffee mixed with roast chicory root, or a dark-roast, Brazilian-based blend without chicory.

Bay Area and Seattle, two regions I know well, blends vary dramatically from roaster to roaster. None is inferior, but their differences can be startling. Experiment and enjoy.

UNBLENDED VARIETAL COFFEES IN ESPRESSO

Unblended varietal coffees consist of beans from one crop and one origin in one country. Most specialty stores carry a small selection of such unblended coffees brought to a dark roast suitable for espresso. They are usually identified by double- and triple-decker names like *Dark Roast Sumatran Lintong, French-Roast Colombian Supremo*, or *Organic Guatemala Antigua Dark*. The intricacies of such multi-leveled names are discussed in the Espresso Break on Coffee Speak on pages 88–91.

In Chapter 5 I briefly described the three broad categories into which traders divide the world's coffees: milds, or quality coffees of the *Coffea arabica* species; Brazils, or mass-processed coffees of the arabica species; and robustas, or coffees of the generally less desirable *Coffea robusta* species.

At present nearly all coffees sold as unblended varietals in North American specialty stores fall into the milds category. For purposes of discussion I would like to further divide the milds category into four subcategories.

First are those coffees that are among the world's rarest, like Ethiopian Yirgacheffe, Yemen Mocha, Sulawesi or Celebes Toraja, Jamaican Blue Mountain, etc. Coffees in this group are seldom dark-roasted because they are relatively expensive, and their subtlety and uniqueness are largely lost in the dark-roasting process.

The second subcategory I would like to propose comprises those coffees that are powerful, rich, and acidy but also widely available, consistent in quality, and not so rare, distinctive, or famous as to demand an exceptional price. The better Guatemalan, Colombian, Kenyan, and Costa Rican coffees might fit this category. Coffees in this subcategory are often offered unblended in a dark-roasted style. Brewed as espresso, they tend to make a rich, interesting, but often overly sharp, imbalanced cup, with untamed acidy notes and a tendency to land heavily on the bitter side of the bittersweet dark-roast taste equation.

The third subcategory of mild coffees I would propose includes those coffees of good quality that lack the rich acidy notes of either of the preceding subcategories, but when dark-roasted show sufficient complexity and richness to satisfy. I would place most quality Mexican, Peruvian, and the better "Santos" coffees of Brazil in this subcategory, together with some of the good but lesser coffees of the Caribbean and Central America. These coffees are occasionally offered in unblended, dark-roasted form. To my taste, they make an excellent espresso, sweeter, smoother, and better balanced than the more acidy coffees described above.

A logical fourth subcategory of mild coffees might include those coffees that contribute richness and body to a blend but without contributing much acidity. The great Indonesian arabica coffees—Sumatran, Celebes or Sulawesi, and the best Estate Java—make a rich, full-bodied espresso with little acidity. Some may find them a bit flat-flavored and lacking tension when drunk unblended as a dark-roast coffee, but to any taste they make an excellent foil for more acidy coffees in an espresso blend. Finally, roasters occasionally offer specially handled coffees like Indian Monsooned Malabar or aged and vintage coffees in a dark-roast preparation. Such coffees make a heavy, dull-flavored espresso on their own, but may be useful in composing personal espresso blends.

BLENDS OF ONE'S OWN

Having sampled some dark-roasted blends and unblended varietals, readers may be interested in experimenting with their own blends. Most specialty stores will be happy to combine coffees for customers, providing the requests don't become too complicated.

To create your own blend, you might start with a base

The open counter of the old Peerless Coffee Company in Oakland, California, an excellent example of the small storefront coffee-roasting establishments that were a familiar feature of North American shopping districts during the nineteenth and early twentieth centuries. A few, like Peerless, survived to join the current revival of specialty coffee roasting. Peerless Coffee, still family-owned, now occupies a large plant a few blocks from its original home.

of dark-roast Mexican or Peruvian, for example, then experiment by asking the clerk to add varying proportions of other beans. Ten percent of a very acidy, winy African coffee like Kenyan plus perhaps another 20 percent of a heavy-bodied coffee like Sumatran or Celebes, both in either a dark or a medium roast, combined with 70 percent dark-roast Mexican or Peruvian, make an interesting and lively blend. Experiment with the proportions of Sumatran and Kenyan until you obtain a balance that satisfies you. For more ideas, look over the blending notes near the end of this chapter.

Those who are not all-out purists may enjoy adding small proportions of flavored beans to a personal espresso blend. Ten percent chocolate- or hazelnut-flavored beans, for example, contributes an interesting flavor note, although the aftertaste may be cloying to an experienced palate.

More Serious Blending

Finally, if you choose to roast your own coffee, there is virtually no end to the possible experiments you can attempt, the only practical limitation being the difficulty you might encounter finding sources for the more exotic green beans. If you need help finding sources for green coffee beans, consult the companion volume to this one, *Coffee: A Guide to Buying, Brewing, and Enjoying*, or write to me, care of the publisher at the address on the copyright page, requesting a list of sources for green beans.

For those who do wish to seriously explore blending for espresso, here are a few final notes on coffees and some of the properties they bring to blends.

Coffees that make a good base, and that add both sweetness and complexity to espresso blends include Mexican wet-processed or washed coffees (Coatepec, the better Chiapas, and Oaxaca) the better wet-processed Peruvian coffees (Chanchamayo, Urubamba, and the best Northerns), and good Haitian and Venezuelan coffees, when they can be found.

Coffees that add body, complexity, and some acidity to blends include Zimbabwe and Hawaiian coffees.

Coffees that add body, complexity, and a sharp acidity to blends include Kenyan, Colombian, and the better Guatemalan and Costa Rican coffees. In addition to complexity and a sharp acidity, Ethiopian Harrar and Yemen coffees contribute a slight wild or earthy twist.

Coffees that add body and richness to blends and that can be used to offset brisker, more acidy coffees include the better Indonesian coffees (Sumatran Mandheling, Celebes or Sulawesi Toraja, and the best Java Estate arabicas).

Coffees that add body to blends and strongly offset more acidy coffees include aged, vintage, and mature coffees, together with Indian Monsooned Malabar.

The best robustas (on the West Coast these are usually Thai robustas; on the East Coast robustas from the Ivory Coast) tend to smooth out a blend, and add sweetness and a rounded, bell-like support to sharper arabicas.

CHAPTER 7

Pressure and Resistance

The Ideal Grind

Grinding Options

Home Grinders

GRINDING AND GRINDERS

Espresso Break

Keeping it Fresh

When one of my coffee books was published in Great Britain, a reviewer for the Manchester Guardian accused me of being "as fussy as a French omelet cook" about coffee. I recognize the cultural bias of the comparison (Do the French accuse one another of being as fussy as an English umbrella-maker, for example?). I am furthermore of the opinion that coffee is considerably more noble and important than omelets, even French omelets. Nevertheless, whenever I find myself about to launch into some detailed set of coffee prescriptions, that accusation comes painfully to mind.

This is one of those moments. To those whose only coffee-making experience has been with brewing methods other than espresso, the remarks I am about to make concerning the importance of the correct grind in espresso brewing will doubtless sound like the mutterings of a French omelet cook, perhaps of an obsessive French omelet cook. So be it, because grinding the coffee may be the single most important act in the entire sequence of espresso-brewing events.

PRESSURE AND RESISTANCE

Recall that the heavy body and rich flavor of espresso coffee are achieved through pressure and resistance: pressure by the brewing water, and resistance to that pressure by a uniform layer of compressed, ground coffee. The hot water, under great pressure, does its best to push its way through the layer of ground coffee, but owing to the resistance of the finely ground and highly compressed coffee, cannot succeed until it has saturated every grain of the coffee, extracting the coffee's entire flavor and perfume almost instantly, and delivering it intact into the cup. This perfectly poised opposition of pressure and resistance is at the heart of the espresso brewing system.

If the grind or the tamping (the distribution and compression of the ground coffee in the filter) is not correct and uniform, the water will simply take the easy route through whatever part of the coffee bed is more coarsely ground or loosely tamped, leaving the more finely ground, correctly tamped portions of coffee out of the process. The result: a watery, underextracted, often bitter cup.

THE IDEAL GRIND

The ideal grind for espresso is 1) a grit just short of powder; 2) a relatively uniform grit in terms of size of grain; and 3) a grit made up of flaked or shaved, rather than torn or compressed, grains.

These three criteria are listed in order of importance. Criterion 1, the proper grind overall, is crucial to any degree of success in espresso brewing. An overly coarse grind will permit the water to gush through the coffee bed and will produce a thin, bitter cup; a powdery grind will slow the brewing process to the point that only dark, burnt-tasting dribbles will escape the filter holder.

However, the optimal grind varies somewhat according to the nature of the brewing apparatus. Larger, more expensive pump and piston machines (categories 4 and 5, pages 111–114) require a finer grind than the relatively inexpensive, steam-pressure apparatus (categories 1 through 3, pages 108–110). The larger machines generate 9 or more atmospheres of pressure, whereas the steam-pressure devices muster only about 1½ atmospheres. The greater the pressure, the finer and more compacted the coffee bed must be to take full advantage of the pressure-resistance equilibrium of the espresso method.

I've already touched on criterion 2, uniform grind. Again, the greater pressure exerted by the machine, the more uniform the grind needs to be. Small steam-pressure machines will make a reasonably flavorful espresso with a relatively inconsistent grind of the kind produced by inexpensive home grinders. The larger pump and piston machines require a much more uniform grind, which can be produced only by a commercial grinder or by one of the more expensive specialized home espresso grinders.

Criterion 3, flaked grains versus torn or crushed grains, may be a typically French-omelet-cook point, yet it remains an important point. There is no doubt that a grind produced by shaving the bean into relatively uniform flakes is superior to a grind produced by crushing the bean or tearing it into irregular pieces. The flaked configuration absorbs water more quickly and completely than the more rounded, compressed grains produced by crushed beans, and more consistently than the irregular grains produced by tearing the beans. Flaked grains are

produced by burr grinders with sharp, high-quality burrs. Torn grains are produced by inexpensive blade grinders, and crushed or compressed grains either by good burr grinders with dull burrs, or by cheap burr grinders whose burrs were dull to start with.

It is true that a grind that is correct and uniform, albeit compressed rather than shaved, will produce decent-quality espresso, but the finest beverage will be produced only by a properly flaked grind.

GRINDING OPTIONS

Ground espresso coffee can be obtained in one of four ways: 1) by buying whole-bean coffees and grinding them at home just before brewing; 2) by buying whole-bean coffees and having them ground on a large-scale commercial machine; 3) by buying pre-ground, canned coffees; 4) by buying espresso "pods," or capsules, little serving-sized paper bags or containers of pre-ground coffee distributed by some equipment manufacturers and designed to fit into their special, proprietary filter holders or filter baskets.

There is no doubt that buying fresh whole-bean coffees, storing them correctly, and grinding them just before brewing produces the freshest and most flavorful coffee of any style, including espresso. The problem with this formula for espresso brewing is the precision required of the grind.

The little electric blade grinders so common now in North American homes, when used with care, will

(continued on page 100)

KEEPING IT
FRESH

Every step of the transformation of green coffee into hot brewed coffee makes the flavor essence of the bean more vulnerable to destruction. Green coffees keep for years, with only a slow, subtle change in flavor. But roasted coffee begins to lose flavor after a week, ground coffee within an hour after grinding, and brewed coffee within minutes.

Espresso and Freshness

One of the many technical superiorities of the espresso system is its emphasis on freshness: Each cup is not only brewed on demand, but the coffee for each cup is *ground* on demand as well. In the finest of traditional Italian caffès, the coffee is also roasted on the premises, pushing the emphasis on freshness to its logical conclusion. For those who are sufficiently enthusiastic and patient to wish to roast their own espresso coffee at home, see pages 55–58 for a brief introduction to that practice.

The Freezer Controversy

Most of us buy our coffee already roasted, however, either in whole-bean form or pre-ground. The question of how to maintain freshness in this fragile substance has produced one of the more vigorous and amusing of pop food debates, with advocates of the "airtight container in a cool, dry place" position doing battle with "keep it in the freezer" advocates, and both attacking the cavalier thoughtlessness of those who simply chuck their coffee into the refrigerator next to the milk and carrots.

The refrigerator position is easiest to demolish. Moisture is the enemy of roasted coffee; the flavor "oils" in roasted coffee are very delicate, volatile water-soluble substances that moisture immediately dilutes and odors taint. Refrigerators tend to be both damp and full of odors. Those who automatically toss anything perishable into the refrigerator upon liberating it from the grocery sack definitely should modify that reflex in regard to coffee.

The airtight-container-in-a-cool-dry-place position makes most sense for coffee that has already been ground, or whole-bean coffee for use on a day-by-day basis. On the other hand, the freezer makes sense for whole-bean coffee that will not be consumed immediately.

Some Informal Experiments

In my admittedly informal experiments, whole-bean coffees placed in a freezer in a sealed container immediately after roasting seem to last for about a month virtually without flavor loss, then begin a slow deterioration. In a few months the flavor loss is clear and dramatic. The oilier, dark-roasted styles of coffee often used in North American espresso cuisine seem to fare worse than somewhat lighter roasts in such tests, although they too seem to hold their flavor for the first month or so.

At any rate, dodging the (doubtless frozen) tomatoes tossed by my opponents in this important debate, I advise readers to buy small lots of freshly roasted coffee and keep that coffee in sealed containers (use *genuinely* sealable containers, the kind with rubber gaskets and clamp-down lids) in a cool, dry place, out of direct sunlight. If, however, you shop for coffee less frequently than the righteous coffee lover truly ought to, and you keep your whole-bean coffee around for more than a week before you consume it, place it in carefully sealed freezer bags in the deepest recesses of your freezer. And when you finally take it out, *leave* it out; in a sealed container in a cool, dry place, naturally.

produce a grind sufficiently fine and uniform to produce decent, albeit thin-bodied, espresso on simple brewing devices that work by steam pressure only (categories 1 through 3, pages 108–110). However, larger pump or piston machines (categories 4 and 5, pages 111–114) require a much more precise grind to operate to their full potential. These machines exert so much pressure on the brewing water that an irregular or slightly coarse grind will permit the water to gush through the coffee far too quickly, resulting in a weak, watery cup. Owners of pump or piston brewers should either purchase one of the more expensive classes of grinders described below under the heading "Home Grinders for Pump and Piston Machines," or purchase their coffee pre-ground. In the latter case, the loss in freshness occasioned by holding pre-ground coffee in storage for a few days will be offset by the superior precision of the grind.

Whole-bean coffees custom-ground in a large, commercial grinder at the point of purchase are the next best alternative to grinding at home. Specialty coffee stores are preferable to supermarkets as a source for such coffees, since specialty stores usually maintain their grinding apparatus better than do supermarkets and stock fresher beans. However, if you do buy at a supermarket or fancy food store and set the grinder yourself, make certain to turn it to the finest setting, usually labeled "espresso." There may be two or three adjustments indicated on the dial for espresso. Set the grinder to the finest of these adjustments unless you are using a stovetop espresso

machine in categories 1 or 2, pages 108–109, in which case use the coarser of the espresso settings.

Canned espresso coffees are a reasonable third alternative if purchased carefully. Some canned coffees are totally inadequate for espresso brewing because they are ground too coarsely. Read the fine print on the can before you buy. If the label says something like "suitable for all brewing methods," return the can to the shelf forthwith. Cans that read "extra fine grind for espresso brewers," or words to that effect, may contain something worth packing in a filter.

From the point of view of freshness, the espresso pods and capsules are the least attractive option. The coffees they contain usually have been roasted and ground in faraway places before being sealed in their little foil or metal packages, and simply will not produce the explosive perfume of espresso brewed from freshly ground, whole-bean coffees. Pods and capsules also represent the most costly way to brew espresso. On the other hand, they do eliminate a good deal of fussing and may be a good approach for beginners or those who use their machines infrequently. For more on pods and capsules in home brewing, see page 128.

HOME GRINDERS

I've divided the various kinds of home grinding apparatus into two categories: those capable of producing a grind sufficiently fine and uniform to use with steam pressure brewers, and those also capable of producing the more

Electric blade grinder

precision grind demanded by higher pressure pump and piston machines.

Home Grinders for Steam-Pressure Brewers

These classes of grinders, *used knowledgeably*, will produce a grind appropriate for the steam-pressure brewers in categories 1 through 3, pages 108–110.

Electric Blade Grinders. These inexpensive, versatile household tools sold for $15 to $25 in 1993. Rather than grinding the coffee between burrs, they whack the coffee to pieces with blades that rotate at a very high speed, like blender blades. These devices also can be used to pulverize spices and softer nuts.

Coffee should be ground in relatively brief bursts. It also helps to gently bounce the bottom of the grinder on the counter between bursts to knock the coffee that often cakes up around the blades or at the edges of the receptacle back down to where the blades can reach it. When you first use a blade grinder for espresso, you will need to regularly check the fineness of the grind. It is usually impossible to visually confirm the correct gritty grind, even with models that provide a sort of magnifying-glass lid. You periodically must stop grinding and pull a pinch out of the receptacle and rub it or look at it. Again,

it should be a fine grit, just short of powder. You can never obtain a perfectly consistent grind with these devices, by the way, so don't waste time trying. When the average particle is grit, carry on with the brewing.

The effort required in getting the ground coffee out from under the blades of these devices also can be trying. However, I find little evidence for another accusation leveled at blade grinders: Some claim that they heat the coffee as they pulverize it, destroying valuable aromatic oils. It is difficult to believe that the (at most) mild warmth these devices impart to coffee while reducing it to a fine grind could have a negative effect on flavor.

Small General-Purpose Electric Burr Grinders. These devices are designed to grind coffee for a variety of brewing methods, and in 1993 retailed for $50 to $90. Rather than whacking the coffee to pieces, they feed the beans between motor-driven, conical burrs; the ground coffee sprays out into the receptacle at the base of the unit. Those that I've tried produce a

General-purpose electric burr grinder

reasonable espresso grind, though not as fine or as uniform a grind as produced by the higher-priced, specialized espresso grinders. Nor are these general-purpose grinders adjustable in as fine increments as are the specialized grinders. Finally, they need to be cleaned even more frequently than do the espresso grinders and in some cases will not feed the oilier dark roasts smoothly. It may be necessary to walk across the kitchen and give the grinder an occasional shake to keep the sticky-surfaced, dark-roast beans moving into the grinding mechanism.

Again, such devices are appropriate only for the low-pressure brewers in categories 1 through 3, pages 108–110. The chief advantage these devices hold over the cheaper blade grinders described earlier is their consistency: Once set to produce a given grind, they will continue to produce that grind until set differently. Unfortunately, the finest setting is still too coarse for the best results with pump or piston machines.

Manual Box Grinders. Box grinders are literally wooden boxes with cranks protruding from the top. As the crank turns, the beans work their way down between two metal cone-shaped burrs, one rotating inside the other. The ground coffee falls into a little drawer at the bottom of the box. Some heavier versions have external metal housings and a flywheel crank on the side, like old-time store grinders.

Manual box grinder

The best and most expensive ($50 and up) of these devices make a consistent, properly flaked espresso grind appropriate for the low-pressure brewers in categories 1 through 3, pages 108–110. In fact, the best of them will produce an acceptable grind even for pump and piston machines if you are patient and don't mind cranking for a minute or two per serving. At the finest setting the beans tend to feed very slowly, which prolongs the grinding process. Still, for those who argue (logically) that the best way to exercise is to do something useful like mow the lawn by hand rather than jog or jump rope, the best of these apparatus might make a reasonable choice for any kind of espresso brewing, including pump and piston.

Home Grinders for Pump and Piston Machines

These classes of grinders will produce a precision grind appropriate for the high-pressure pump and piston brewers in categories 4 and 5, pages 111–114.

Specialized Electric Burr Grinders Designed for Espresso Brewing. If you are pursuing a true caffè-quality espresso, you will need to pony up the $100 to $250 required for a proper, specialized espresso grinder. These devices flake the coffee properly and are adjustable in fine enough increments so that aficionados can fine-tune their grind setting to accommodate changes in ambient humidity and moisture content in the beans.

The majority of these grinders also include a

spring-loaded doser, a device that dispenses a serving's worth (a dose) of ground coffee with a flick of a lever. Some also include an attached tamper to distribute and press the coffee into the filter.

Both of these features are useful, provided they match the filter holder and filter of the machine you own or intend to purchase. Dosers have a cradle-like device that holds the filter holder in position to receive the dose of ground coffee. Make sure that you try out the filter holder from the machine you own or intend to own to make certain that it fits the doser cradle of the grinder you are considering buying. Surprising mismatches occur, even between grinders and machines from the same manufacturer.

As for the tamper, its general bottom profile and overall diameter should match the bottom profile and diameter of the filter from your machine. If not, continue to use the tamper that the manufacturer of your machine provided.

A specialized espresso grinder may be a useful purchase even if the doser offers the wrong fit for your machine's filter holder, since most of the grinders in this class provide the option of replacing the doser with a lidded receptacle (included with the grinder), from which you simply spoon the coffee into the filter.

Manual Grain Mills. Grain mills are designed for those who prefer to grind their own flour. Grain mills with *metal* (not stone) grinding plates produce a uniform, properly gritty espresso grind, although some espresso enthusiasts claim that conical burrs produce a flakier grind

than do flat plates, because the former shave the coffee, whereas the plates tend to crush and compress it.

In 1993 only one good manual grain mill was available in the United States, the Jupiter, which sold for around $90. The Corona, a less expensive mill, should not be used to grind coffee owing to its poor-quality grinding plates. Although grain mills offer a relatively inexpensive alternative to specialized electric espresso grinders, they are messy to use and require a strong arm, a sturdy table, and a good deal of kitchen space.

Electric burr grinder, specially designed for espresso brewing. The cylinder at the front of the device is a doser, or ground coffee dispenser.

ESPRESSO AT HOME: BREWING APPARATUS

Espresso Break

From Pot to Machine: Home Espresso Apparatus

*S*ooner or later those who enjoy espresso at caffès and bars begin to think about making their own espresso drinks at home. For many the prospect may appear intimidating. The caffè machines are large, complex, and obviously expensive, and involve the use of steam under so much pressure that it literally explodes out of the wands used to froth milk.

Home espresso brewing, although more complex than many culinary procedures, is not difficult in the long run. It does require some patience, however, both in the selection of gear and in mastering the various procedures. As in most undertakings dependent on technology, the more you spend on equipment, the fewer details you need to master. Nevertheless, even those prepared to spend large sums of money on the best apparatus need to master some procedure, as well as understand the principles behind that procedure. Espresso is still an undertaking in which excellence needs to be learned, rather than simply bought.

This chapter and the related Espresso Break on brewing equipment (pages 108–114) offer an orientation to various classes of home espresso brewing equipment and some advice on choosing that equipment. If you already own satisfactory espresso apparatus, skip to Chapter 9 and related Espresso Breaks for some advice and encouragement on using it.

DECIDING WHAT YOU WANT

The first step in buying an espresso brewing system is deciding what you like about espresso and how much you are willing to spend to achieve it at home.

For example, if you simply like the bittersweet tang of dark-roasted coffee and can do without the rich, heavy body of espresso-style coffee and the hot frothed milk used in many popular espresso drinks, then you can get by very cheaply. All you need do is buy some dark-roasted coffee and make it in your drip brewer as you would with any other coffee.

Or, if you simply like the large, milky drink usually called *caffè latte*, you do need specialized apparatus, but by espresso standards it can be relatively inexpensive apparatus. The under-$100 brewing devices in category 3, page 110, used with an inexpensive blade grinder, and *used knowledgeably*, will produce a satisfying caffè latte or latte macchiato. Such relatively inexpensive apparatus will not produce the true, classic cappuccino or a satisfying demitasse of straight espresso topped with golden crema, however. For those drinks you need something resembling the larger household machines described in categories 4 and 5 on pages 111–114. You also need precision-ground coffee, produced either by a specialized home espresso grinder (see Chapter 7) or by a commercial grinder.

For those who are deeply attracted to the romance and mystique of espresso, or who entertain often and on a large scale, or who are contemplating outfitting a small office with espresso capability, a complete high-end system is a necessity, including specialized grinder with doser, and a heavy-duty, refillable pump machine with cup warmer (high end of category 4, pages 111–112). A fully automatic machine (also high end of category 4) is another attractive possibility for those outfitting small offices, or who entertain heavily.

Once you have an idea of what your goal is, you might familiarize yourself with the various categories of brewing equipment described on pages 108–114, then glance over the discussion that follows on various points of comparison among competing designs within each category.

CATEGORY 1:
SIMPLE STOVETOP BREWERS

These little devices, described and illustrated on pages 108–109, produce a rather thin-bodied beverage closer to strong drip or French-press coffee than to true espresso. Furthermore, they do not offer milk-frothing capacity.

Category 1: "Moka"-Style Designs

The clearest point of comparison among the hourglass-shaped "Moka"-style pots (see page 108) is the material used in the top part of the pot, which receives the freshly brewed coffee as it sputters up through the filter. The best of these designs use ceramic or glass for this part of

the pot; the next best use stainless steel; the worst use aluminum. Aluminum, and to a lesser degree stainless steel, become so hot that the metal burns the first dribbles of brewed coffee, often spoiling the taste of the entire batch. Some versions of this design make the ceramic, coffee-receiving part of the device removable, so that it can be lifted off the rest of the pot and taken to the table.

The other point of comparison among the Moka-style pots is appearance. The international design community has been loosed on these devices. In 1993, designer versions of the Moka-style pots cost up to $200 and are among the most visually elegant of coffee-making apparatus. Keep in mind, however, that regardless of looks and price, all of the Moka-style pots work the same way.

Category 1: Other Designs

Designs that deliver the coffee directly into the cup are a good idea; the cup (see page 109, top) is automatically pre-warmed and the coffee is not burned by contact with hot metal. The style of pot illustrated on page 109, center has two additional advantages: First, the filter receptacle that holds the ground coffee is set off to the side of the water reservoir, which means one can apply more heat to the water without baking the ground coffee; and second, the caffè-style filter receptacle can be removed without disassembling the pot, which makes it easier to recharge the device with ground coffee when brewing multiple servings.

(continued on page 115)

From Pot to Machine: Home Espresso Apparatus

Home brewing devices for espresso range from the modest little stove-top apparatus Italians call caffettiere, or "coffeepots," that in 1993 retailed for as little as $15, to fully automatic devices that produce espresso virtually equal to the best caffè production at the press of a button and at this writing cost as much as $900. Most home espresso brewing devices fall between these extremes of price and capability. For purposes of analysis I've divided them into five categories.

CATEGORY I

Simple Stovetop Brewers

Without Valve for Frothing and Heating Milk;

Without Mechanism for Controlling Coffee Output

Brewing pressure supplied by natural build-up of steam pressure trapped in boiler.

Advantages. Some designs are very inexpensive; others are very attractive.

Disadvantages. Cannot produce espresso drinks using frothed milk; require great care to produce even passable espresso; can only brew multiple servings.

These little devices are not true espresso brewers; unless used with the greatest care, they produce a thin, bitter, over-extracted coffee that only an Italian could love, and not for very long if there is an espresso bar around.

The most familiar profile is the hour-glass design called a *Moka-style* pot, on the left, after the model name for the most famous and widely distributed of the brewers using this design. The illustration provides a cutaway view

Moka-style pot

Stovetop pot brewing directly into cup

Stovetop pot incorporating caffè-style filter holder

Stovetop brewer with frothing wand

of such a device. The water boils in the bottom part of the pot (A); the pressure of the trapped steam forces hot water up a tube and through the ground coffee held in a metal filter at the waist of the pot (B); the brewed coffee trickles out into the receptacle at the top of the pot (C).

All of the various designs illustrated here, as well as those described in later pages in categories 2 and 3, work in similar fashion, using the same pressure of trapped steam to force the brewing water through the coffee. All provide a brewing pressure of about 1 ½ to 3 atmospheres, considerably less than the 9 or more atmospheres now considered optimal for espresso brewing.

Designs like the example illustrated at the top brew the coffee directly into the cup; and designs like the device in the center brew into a separate receptacle and make use of an external, caffè-style filter holder and filter.

CATEGORY 2

Stovetop Brewers with Frothing Wand

With Valve for Frothing and Heating Milk;

With Mechanism for Controlling Coffee Output

Brewing pressure supplied by natural build-up of steam pressure trapped in boiler.

Advantages. Inexpensive; easy to store; operated carefully, can produce acceptable espresso drinks with frothed milk; can be used to froth milk or prepare hot beverages independent of the coffee-making operation.

Disadvantages. Cannot produce authentic straight espresso; require care to produce espresso acceptable for frothed milk drinks; can brew only multiple servings.

These devices are identical in operation to the category 1 brewers but add a steam valve and wand for heating and frothing milk, and a valve for controlling coffee output. These designs, once popular, have now largely been supplanted on the North American market by designs described in category 3.

Countertop Steam Pressure Brewers

With Valve for Frothing and Heating Milk;

With Mechanism for Controlling Coffee Output

Brewing pressure supplied by natural build-up of steam pressure trapped in boiler.

Advantages. Inexpensive; provide more predictable, stable steam pressure than stovetop models in categories 1 and 2. Operated carefully, can produce acceptable espresso drinks with frothed milk; can be used to froth milk or prepare hot beverages independent of the coffee-making operation.

Disadvantages. Cannot produce authentic straight espresso; require care to produce espresso acceptable for frothed milk drinks; occupy some counter space.

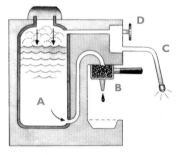

Countertop steam pressure brewer

Devices of this design are currently the most popular of espresso brewers on the North American market. They operate on the same principle as the category 1 and 2 devices but add an electric heating element, which promotes a more consistent and safer steam pressure. See the cross-section illustration on the left. The closed boiler (A) generates steam, which forces the hot water below it out and through the ground coffee in the filter and filter holder at (B). The steam wand (C) controlled by a steam valve (D) taps the steam for milk frothing.

These brewers are designed to provide the North American "latte" and casual cappuccino drinker with an adequate drink at a reasonable price. In 1993 they retailed between $50 and $100. All provide a steam valve and wand for frothing and heating milk. All have an aluminum boiler with stainless steel filter and filter holder. All separate the filter and filter holder from the boiler to avoid overheating the ground coffee, and all have a removable, caffè-style filter and filter holder.

Cross-section, countertop steam pressure brewer

Countertop Pump Machines

With Valve for Frothing and Heating Milk;

Switch-Activated Pump System Controls Coffee Output

Brewing pressure supplied by pump. Approximate pressure 6 to 15 atmospheres.

Advantages. Make near-caffè quality espresso and espresso drinks with frothed milk if used correctly; refillable reservoirs make it possible to produce any number of espresso drinks without interruption or cool-down; achieve brewing temperature relatively rapidly; unlike all other categories of machine, brew with water held at optimal (lower-than-boiling) brewing temperature.

Disadvantages. Take up counter space; more expensive than category 3 devices; more reticent and less romantic in appearance and operation than category 5 machines; unlike category 5 machines require a transitional procedure between brewing and frothing; in some cases less sturdy than category 5 machines.

At this point we enter the world of the true home espresso machine. All of the devices in this and the following category provide means to press the hot water through the coffee bed at pressures considerably exceeding the 1½ to 3 atmospheres generated by stream pressure alone. All provide steam valves and wands; all utilize separate caffè-style filters and filter holders that can be repeatedly charged with ground coffee for multiple "pulls" of one to two servings of espresso each.

The designs in this category provide additional pressure on the hot water by means of an electric pump; a separate function provides steam for milk-frothing. The separation of brewing and frothing functions permits the brewing water to be delivered to the coffee at the approximately 186° to 192°F authorities agree is optimal for espresso brewing. Designs in all of the other categories deliver the water at near boiling temperature, since the same function that delivers steam for the frothing operation also delivers hot water for brewing. Boiling water tends to extract many of the bitterish chemicals in the coffee along with the desirable flavor volatiles.

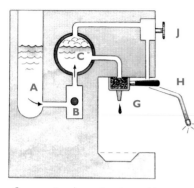

Cross-section, home pump machine

Typical home pump machine

In almost all pump machines the operator is asked to first brew the coffee, then activate a switch or hold down a button, which raises the heat in the boiler or heating coil from the lower brewing temperature to a higher temperature appropriate for steam production.

Internal Elements. The principal concealed elements of pump machines are indicated in the cross-section illustration on the left: a water reservoir (A), in which the water is held at room temperature and which can be refilled while the machine is in use; an electric pump (B) for transferring water from reservoir to boiler, and for pressing the brewing water through the coffee; a small boiler (C) for heating water for brewing and steam production; and various control mechanisms, including two thermostats, one for controlling the heat applied to the water during brewing, and one for controlling the considerably higher heat applied to the water during the production of steam for milk frothing.

External Elements. The external features (see photograph on the left) mimic the features of the large caffè machines. They include (D) an opening for servicing the water reservoir; (E) a gauge to indicate water level in the reservoir; (F) the brewing group, into which the filter holder clamps; (G) the filter holder and the filter basket; (H) the steam wand or pipe; (I) the steam nozzle used to froth milk; (J) the knob or switch for controlling the steam pressure for the milk-frothing operation; (K) the controls, usually including a power switch and switches that activate the brewing and steam functions; and (L) the drip tray. Some designs, like the one pictured, may also include a cup-warming shelf (M) atop the machine and a built-in tamper (N).

Fully Automatic Machines. Some home pump machines are beginning to appear in the North American market that, like many of the newer caffè machines, brew coffee automatically, at the touch of a button. See page 33, bottom for a photograph of such a machine. A series of mechanisms inside the machine grinds the coffee, loads it, tamps it, presses the appropriate volume of water through the ground coffee, and finally drops the spent grounds into a removable waste container, all at the touch of a button. For drinks with frothed milk the operator must still froth the milk and assemble the drink, however.

Countertop Piston Machines

With Valve for Frothing and Heating Milk;

Hand-Operated Piston Controls Coffee Output

Brewing pressure supplied by spring-loaded or hand-operated piston. Brewing pressure supplied by the piston will vary, but will considerably exceed the pressure supplied by trapped steam in the category 1 through 3 devices.

Advantages. Make near-caffè quality espresso and espresso drinks with frothed milk if used correctly; sturdier in construction than all but the most expensive category 4 machines; more conversation-provoking in appearance and operation than category 4 machines; more silent than category 4 machines (no pump noise); require no transitional procedure between brewing and frothing; offer more finely tuned control of brewing pressure than category 4 machines.

Disadvantages. Take up counter space; expensive; slower to warm up than category 4 machines; must be turned off and bled of steam pressure before refilling; boiler is exposed in most machines, and hot to the touch; may not provide as strong a brewing pressure as category 4 machines; brewing water is hotter than optimal brewing temperature maintained by category 4 machines.

Typical home piston machine

The sometimes hard-to-find machines in this category are piston machines, in which the additional pressure applied to the brewing water is delivered by a piston fitted into a cylinder, much as it is in the large piston machines still in use in many North American caffès. The piston first lifts, drawing water into the cylinder below the piston and above the bed of ground coffee, then sinks, pressing the water down through the coffee.

At least one currently available machine in this category has a spring-loaded piston similar in design to the large manual caffè machines. A lever is depressed, compressing a spring above the piston; the spring then presses piston and water down, while the

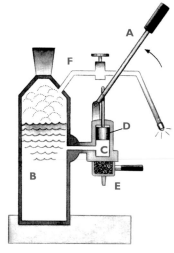

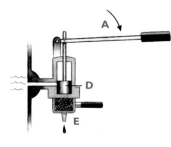

Cross-section home piston machine

lever handle slowly returns to its original upright position. See an illustration of such a mechanism on page 113.

However, most of the machines available in this category use the simple muscle power of the operator to provide the pressure on the water. See the illustration showing a cross-section of a typical home manual piston machine. First the operator raises the lever (A), drawing water from the boiler (B) into the cylinder (C). Next the operator leans on the lever, forcing the piston (D) down, and the brewing water through the filter holder and coffee at (E). Steam for milk frothing is provided by tapping the top of the boiler with the usual wand and valve (F).

Unlike the semiautomatic pump machines in category 4, these designs hold the water for both milk-frothing and coffee-brewing in the same large reservoir. This arrangement involves several drawbacks. First, the water must be held at a high enough temperature to provide steam pressure for frothing, which means it is hotter than the approximate 190° F authorities agree is optimal for espresso brewing. Secondly, one needs to wait for the entire reservoir to heat up before beginning to brew, a procedure that may take up to fifteen minutes. Finally, one must cool the entire machine before refilling the water reservoir. The semiautomatic pump machines in category 4 can be refilled while in use.

The great advantages to these machines are their solid construction and romantic appearance. Also some aficionados prefer to apply manual pressure to the brewing water because they feel that they can fine-tune the brewing pressure to compensate for variations in fineness of grind and the effects of humidity on the resistance of the coffee.

Home piston machines are often difficult to find. If you need help identifying a source, consult Finding Espresso Coffee and Equipment, pages 169–170.

CATEGORY 2: STOVETOP WITH FROTHING WAND

These are stove-top brewers like those in category 1, but with valve and wand for frothing milk. See the illustration and description on page 109. In 1993 examples of this style of brewer could be found selling for $40 to $90. They provide roughly the same capability as the countertop electrics in category 3, although the category 3 brewers are more widely available and easier to use.

The great drawback of these stovetop devices is the filter design: The ground coffee usually is held in a filter *inside* the machine. Brewers like the category 3 designs that use caffè-style filter holders that clamp onto the outside of the machine have several advantages over category 3 brewers: They enable you to brew one or two cups at a time rather than an entire pot; you can use a finer grind of coffee; and you can reload the brewer for another round of coffee-making without taking it entirely apart.

The main point of comparison among the current crop of these brewers is material. Stainless steel is superior to aluminum.

CATEGORY 3: COUNTERTOP STEAM PRESSURE

These steam-pressure brewers, like the category 2 devices, incorporate a steam valve and wand for frothing milk, but the heat is provided by a built-in electric element. See page 110 for an illustrated description. The main points of comparison among these popular devices:

Coffee Control. The best of these devices incorporate a switch or other means to cut off the flow of coffee. I would not purchase a brewer without this function, which is essential, both as a means for timing the brewing operation to prevent overextracted coffee and as a way of diverting all of the accumulated pressure in the boiler to the milk-frothing operation once the brewing procedure is finished.

Steam Control. The best of these devices also have an adjustable, screw-type steam valve, which permits one to modulate the strength of the steam flow for fine-tuned control of the milk-frothing and heating operation. Some designs control the steam function with a simple on-off switch.

Special Milk-frothing Nozzles. Some designs seek to assist the novice milk-frother by adding various special nozzles to the end of the steam wand. All of these gadgets are essentially aerating devices that introduce room-temperature air into the coffee along with the steam. They are a mixed blessing. Although they assist in the milk-frothing operation, they complicate clean-up. See the Espresso Break on milk frothing, pages 135–139.

CATEGORY 4: COUNTERTOP PUMP MACHINES

Devices in this category are genuine espresso "machines"; used properly they will produce a genuine tazzina of espresso: rich, sweet, almost syrupy in weight, and topped with a dense-textured head of golden crema. They all use a pump to drive the brewing water through the tightly packed coffee; they all provide milk-frothing apparatus; and, except for those very expensive machines that are entirely automatic and do everything at the touch of a button, including grinding, loading, and tamping the coffee, they all use a detachable, caffè-style filter and filter holder.

The many machines in this category offer a very wide range of features, comparison points, and prices. They can be loosely divided into three subcategories: lighter-weight, smaller machines that in 1993 sold for approximately $150 to $300; heavier, larger machines that sold for about $350 to $700; and completely automatic machines that retailed for $650 to $900. I will add a few words at the end of this section on the fully automatic machines. The points of comparison outlined below apply to distinctions among the many conventional, semiautomatic pump machines.

Category 4: General Points of Comparison

Materials and weight together constitute one of the main points that distinguish higher- from lower-priced designs. Weight is not simply a psychological factor; the heavier the machine the less likely it is to slide away when clamping the filter holder into the group. Italians call such lightweight machines *macchine ballanti*, "dancing machines."

Weight and Material. In the higher-priced machines the boiler is usually constructed of brass (unless the heating is accomplished by a coil in what usually is called a *thermal block* unit); in the lower-priced machines the boiler is usually made of aluminum. In the higher-priced machines the group and filter holder are heavy and fit together authoritatively; in less-expensive machines both may be a bit on the flimsy, "dancing" side. In the finest machines the housing is made of metal; in lower-to-medium-priced machines, it is constructed of varying weights of plastic.

Transition Between Brewing and Frothing. The complexity and convenience of the transition between brewing and frothing functions may also be a point of comparison. Some machines require the operator to hold down a button for up to 30 seconds; others require only pressing a switch, and accomplish the transition in half that time.

Water Reservoir. The water reservoir is removable in most machines, which simplifies refilling. A few of the smaller machines may have built-in reservoirs, a minor inconvenience.

Filter Catch. Most machines provide a means for keeping the filter inside the filter holder when the spent grounds are knocked out in preparation for charging the filter with another dose of ground coffee. This is a small but important feature. A few machines may not have it at all; others may incorporate a little flap that needs to be held down manually. The best filter catches utilize magnets, spring clips, or sliding tabs; the filter remains secure during brewing but pops out easily for cleaning, or for switching to another filter with larger or smaller capacity.

Other External Features. External design aspects vary. Some machines have a deep, removable drip tray that accommodates a good deal of waste liquid and can be lifted out of the machine for dumping and cleaning. Other machines have a smallish drip tray that requires the operator to either unplug the machine and carry it to the sink, or sop up the waste liquid with repeated passes of a sponge. The steam wand of some machines is awkwardly placed, with the nozzle too close to counter or drip tray to permit easy access for a milk-frothing pitcher. This design failure can be particularly infuriating for North Americans who take their espresso with large quantities of milk, and who may find themselves indulging in odd kitchen acrobatics to extricate full milk pitchers out from under strangely placed steam wands.

Category 4: Special Features

A somewhat bewildering variety of special features also distinguishes these machines, although many constitute minor enhancements or conveniences rather than major points of comparison.

Milk-frothing and Crema-Promoting Gadgets. Various devices that fit on the steam wand to make milk frothing easier are described on pages 135–136. Some machines also have special filter holders that improve production of crema, the pale gold froth that covers the surface of a well-made tazzina of straight espresso. For those who prefer their espresso straight, without frothed milk, these crema-enhancing devices may be an important feature. All of the category 4 machines, used properly will produce some crema, but these special filter holders assure success. For more on the crema issue, see the Espresso Break on pages 132–134.

Espresso Pods and Capsules. In an effort to simplify the grinding, loading, and tamping procedure, some home espresso machine manufacturers have developed proprietary systems that enable the consumer to brew with prepackaged, ready-to-brew, single servings of precision-ground coffee. In the simpler of these systems, the coffee is contained in single-serving, flow-through bags usually called "pods." (Public relations departments aspire to fancier names; one manufacturer calls them "Kisses".) You pop one or two pods (or kisses) into a special, proprietary filter basket that comes with your machine and brew away.

A similar but more elaborate system uses "capsules," sealed disposable single-serving metal containers of pre-ground coffee that fit directly into a special filter holder, replacing the usual filter basket. The capsules have pressure-sensitive seals that pop open and deliver the coffee when the water pressure reaches the optimum level for brewing. Current machines using capsules can brew only with capsules; "pod" machines usually give you the option of using an ordinary filter basket, should you tire of pods and wish to brew with ordinary bulk or canned coffee.

Manufacturers may develop similar systems in the future. All will doubtless be very helpful for beginners. However, unless these systems offer the option of conventional brewing as well as brewing assisted by pods, capsules, or whatever, they will prove costly over the long haul for those who drink a good deal of espresso. Pre-ground coffee delivered in proprietary single-serving containers inevitably costs more than coffee purchased in bulk.

Water Softeners. Calcium build-up from hard water can disable these machines by clogging the pump and other components. At least two machines available at this writing have built-in water-softening devices. Of course you can always either decalcify the machine on a regular basis or brew with bottled water.

Cup Warmers. Some machines also come with cup warmers, which are useful, particularly for straight espresso drinkers. The little cups used for espresso must be pre-warmed or they will cool the coffee and shrink the head of crema. Caffè latte and cappuccino drinkers have less to be concerned about in this regard, since the hot frothed milk partly compensates for the cooling impact of glass or cup.

Anti-drip Mechanisms. The group on most pump machines has an annoying tendency to leak slightly when the power is on. Some machines incorporate anti-drip mechanisms intended to alleviate this minor incontinence.

Other Features. Finally, some machines incorporate various amenities like accessory drawers, built-in tampers, and little knock-out drawers for spent grounds. I prefer tampers built into the machine to the usual hand-held tampers, since I find them easier to use. Many espresso fanatics will only use a hand-held tamper, however, because it facilitates the twisting motion that polishes the surface of the charge of ground coffee. Built-in knock-out drawers for spent grounds would be useful if they weren't usually too flimsy to take a good knock.

Category 4: A Summary of Points of Comparison

Consider these points in comparing semiautomatic pump machines:

- How heavy is the machine? Does it have a brass boiler and metal housing? Does it appear to be sturdy enough to stand up to the use you intend for it?
- Is the transitional procedure for moving between brewing coffee and frothing milk more lengthy or more cumbersome than the similar procedure in other machines?
- Is there an adequate catch to hold the filter in the filter holder when one knocks out spent grounds?
- If the machine offers a gadget approach to milk frothing, is it possible to remove the gadget if you wish to froth milk in the conventional manner? Is the steam control adjustable, or do you simply turn it on? (Adjustable is better.) Is the steam wand easy to access?
- Is the drip tray shallow and fixed, or deep and removable? (Deep and removable is better.)
- Do you find other features of the machine attractive?
- Is the seller well-established in your area? Has the seller been handling espresso machines for some

time, and do the sales personnel appear to understand them? What sort of service arrangement does your seller offer?

- When demonstrated for you, does the machine brew and assemble satisfactory drinks of the kind you look forward to enjoying? Does the machine drip excessively when the power is on and the brewing function turned off?

Of course, all of these features need to be weighed against cost; many of us find it easy to tolerate a few missing features or awkward design solutions in a machine that costs a couple of hundred dollars less than its competitors and makes equally good coffee.

Category 4: Fully Automatic Pump Machines

Because so few of these machines are imported to North America, I am treating them as a subcategory of the pump machines in category 4. Calling them "fully automatic" may be somewhat misleading to a North American caffè latte drinker. What is fully automated is the coffee-making procedure. The operator still needs to froth the milk and combine it with the coffee to produce drinks like caffè latte and cappuccino. These devices start with a standard pump machine and build into it a coffee-grinding unit similar to the specialized home espresso grinders described in Chapter 7, together with a mechanism that, at the touch of a button, does all of the fussy little things necessary to producing good espresso: It

grinds the coffee, packs it into the filter, starts and stops the brewing, and dumps the spent grounds.

The main points of comparison for these machines are reliability and ease of cleaning. Make certain that the clerk demonstrates the machine before you buy, that you taste the espresso, and that everything appears to operate as described. Having made certain that the machine operates well, have the clerk demonstrate how easy or difficult the brewing mechanism is to clean. The market leader in this category in Europe has prevailed over its rivals because its machines are simple, reliable, and above all, incorporate a brewing mechanism that pulls out easily for flushing under a faucet.

CATEGORY 5: COUNTERTOP PISTON MACHINES

Those who choose one of these romantically old-fashioned devices (see page 113 for a description and illustration) love their appearance and charming directness, and value their solidity. Their silent, simple operation keeps them out of the shop longer than most pump machines, and used knowledgeably they produce espresso as good as any.

In 1993, machines in this category retailed for $400 to $700, depending on the following points of comparison:

Boiler Capacity. Since these devices need to be cooled down before being refilled, and once refilled take 10 minutes or more to achieve brewing temperature, a large capacity boiler may be a distinct advantage.

Thermostatic Control. The more expensive machines in this category incorporate a thermostat that adjusts heat in the boiler so that the machine can be left on for prolonged periods, sparing you the long wait for the machine to heat up, and probably saving on energy costs as well.

Piston mechanism. At this writing one machine in this class offers a true spring-loaded piston mechanism, whereas others simply use the muscle-power of the operator to force the brewing water through the coffee.

Appearance. The romantic appearance of these devices, with their pipes, valves, and levers, is one of the main reasons many people prefer them to the more reticent-looking pump machines. Manufacturers cater to this appeal by adding fancy finishes and exotic ornament to some models, including gold plate, brass eagles, etc.

CHAPTER 9

ASSEMBLING THE DRINKS

A look at the list of beverages in the classic and contemporary American or Seattle espresso cuisines given on pages 39–40, 43–48 is an excellent place to start in assembling drinks at home. Remember, however, that much of the jargon attached to the various caffè drinks may be irrelevant in your kitchen, where the goal is simply to produce something you and your guests will enjoy, regardless of what it is called.

Before assembling espresso drinks, you may wish to look through the Espresso Breaks on selecting coffee (pages 88–91), brewing the coffee (pages 126–129), and frothing the milk (pages 135–139).

INGREDIENTS AND RECEPTACLES

Milk. Classic espresso cuisine uses ordinary whole milk for drinks like cappuccino and caffè latte. However, North Americans have pressed virtually every other liquid dairy and pseudo-dairy product into use: nonfat milk, one-percent milk, two-percent milk, extra-rich milk, half-and-half, whipping cream, soy milk, and commercial eggnog. With the proper technique, all will froth nicely, though the fattier versions of milk may be somewhat easier to froth for the beginner. To my taste, skimmed (nonfat) milk is too watery, and whipping cream too flat and fatty-tasting for the frothed component of the espresso cuisine. I suggest you try whole milk first and work your way up or down in fat content from there.

Whipped Cream. The whipped cream used in the best North American and Italian caffès is never canned and seldom sweetened. A generous dollop of it is laid on top of the drink. Customers then sweeten to taste. I suggest you begin as the caffès do, with proper whipped cream, unsweetened. You can always turn to substitutes for reasons of diet or convenience later, after you have experienced the basic cuisine.

FLAVORINGS AND GARNISHES

The flavorings used in espresso cuisine can be usefully divided into five categories:

- Traditional, "natural" flavorings used in the classic cuisine: the lemon peel in espresso Romano and the chocolate concentrate in the caffè Mocha, for example.
- Various garnishes sprinkled over frothed milk: in the traditional cuisine unsweetened chocolate and possibly cinnamon, but in the contemporary North American cuisine a variety of other powders and spices, some sweetened and some not.
- Concentrated, unsweetened liquid flavorings: either "extracts" designed for cooking, or similarly concentrated flavoring liquids intended specifically for use with coffee.
- Flavored whole-bean coffees: the Hazelnut-Vanillas, Chocolate Rums, and Irish Cremes of the specialty coffee world.
- Italian-style syrups originally designed to flavor soft drinks, but increasingly used to flavor caffè latte and other espresso drinks made with frothed milk.

Flavorings in the Traditional Cuisine. The only flavorings the classic cuisine proposes are simple to the point of austerity: a twist of lemon peel with straight espresso (*espresso Romano*), a dash of unsweetened chocolate powder over the frothed milk of a cappuccino, or a serving of concentrated hot chocolate in the Italian-American caffè Mocha. In wildly experimental moments, the purist may substitute a twist of orange or tangerine peel for the lemon, or sprinkle cinnamon instead of chocolate on a cappuccino.

The chocolate powder used in the traditional cuisine should be unsweetened but as powerful and perfumy as possible. Most coffee specialty stores now sell a good version of this ingredient. A recipe for the concentrated hot chocolate used in the traditional caffè Mocha is given later in this chapter under the heading for that drink.

Garnishes. Garnishes sprinkled over the head of frothed milk that covers the surfaces of drinks like cappuccino and caffè latte have become a ubiquitous part of North American espresso cuisine. They originated with the Italian practice of garnishing cappuccino with a light dusting of unsweetened chocolate powder, but North Americans now have extended the practice to include most drinks made with frothed milk and an increasing variety of spices and flavorings.

The unsweetened chocolate of the Italian cuisine is often replaced by a sweetened chocolate, for example, and some use Mexican chocolate, a sweetened, spiced chocolate sold in cake form that must be grated over the frothed milk. Still others prefer to grate or shave baking chocolate—unsweetened, semi-sweet or white—over their frothed milk drinks. At least one accessory manufacturer offers a handsome device expressly designed to grate baking and other hard chocolate over espresso drinks. Any good cheese grater will do the job, however.

To my knowledge cinnamon is never used in Italy to garnish coffee. It has a long history in North American spiced coffee drinks, however, so it inevitably made an early appearance as a garnish in the American espresso cuisine. For my part, I don't like cinnamon with espresso; I find that it doesn't harmonize with the dark tones of the coffee.

Like everything else about the exuberant contemporary American, or Seattle-style espresso cuisine, garnishes know no limits. At one Seattle espresso cart I counted twelve garnishes available for patrons to sprinkle over their frothed-milk drinks, including sweetened and unsweetened chocolate powders, vanilla powder, orange powder, cinnamon, powdered nutmeg, and fresh nutmeg (presented with grater). The cart owner claimed that one man used every one of these garnishes on his caffè latte. This variety is possible in part because garnishing powders especially designed for espresso cuisine are beginning to become available at specialty coffee and fancy food stores. These garnishes come in shaker-top bottles in a range of sweetened and unsweetened forms. Of those I've tried the only one that has impressed me is the unsweetened vanilla, but if you like variety carry on.

Unsweetened Concentrate Flavorings. Adding a few drops of unsweetened, concentrated flavor extract—vanilla, almond, orange—to espresso appears to have been an unusual but not unheard-of practice in earlier decades of the espresso cuisine in the United States. The notion has been given a boost in recent years, however, by the success of flavored whole-bean coffees, the hazelnut cremes, Irish cremes, chocolate raspberries, and so on, that have made their fragrant appearance in specialty coffee stores over the past fifteen years. Flavored whole-bean coffees, by the way, are decent but ordinary coffees, brought to a medium roast, then coated with a variety of flavoring agents. The flavorings are drawn from the repertoire developed for soft drinks and other processed foods, modified for use with coffee.

Within the past few years various merchandisers have hit on the obvious—why not add the flavorings to the coffee *after* it has been brewed, rather than before? Consequently, we now have lines of unsweetened flavorings sold in little pocket- or purse-sized bottles, bearing the same exotic names as the flavored whole-bean coffees: hazelnut creme, macadamia, pineapple coconut, chocolate mint, etc. These products join the similar but more traditional flavor extracts originally designed for cooking: vanilla, almond, and so on.

Those who don't care to take their espresso drinks with sugar but wish to experiment with flavorings might try one of these products. Most use "natural" flavor extracts in an alcohol-and-water base. Some use propylene glycol in their base, a substance whose presence has disturbed some of the health-conscious among us. Propylene glycol is widely used in prepared foods and has never been implicated by any study of disease-causing agents, but for those who wish to avoid it, there are still many flavorings that use only alcohol and water as a base, and a few (usually found in natural food stores) that use only water.

Flavored Whole-Bean Coffees. Another way to subtly flavor straight espresso is to add a few flavored beans (not over 25 percent) to an espresso blend before grinding. The flavoring materials added to such whole-bean coffees can cumulatively clog and taint burr coffee grinders, however, so if you do add flavored beans to an espresso blend, you might have the blend ground at the store. I find liquid concentrate flavorings far more attractive than flavored whole beans for enhancing straight espresso. Flavored whole-bean coffees tend to add a flat, chemical aftertaste to the cup, a taint that is considerably less pronounced with the concentrate flavorings.

Flavored Syrups. It was inevitable that the Italian-style fountain syrups that for so many years spread their tantalizing rainbow of colors and flavors across the back bars of caffès would break out of their limited role as soft-drink flavors and begin to find their way into coffee drinks. They are usually used to flavor tall, milky drinks rather than straight espresso, where more subtlety is called for. The flavored caffè latte in particular has become a Seattle espresso cart staple: Italian-style syrups are added to a freshly brewed caffè latte, making it a hazelnut latte, a raspberry latte, and on into the multi-flavored latte sunset. Several brands of flavored syrup, made in both the United States and Europe, now compete with the widely distributed Torani line. If you try one of these syrups at home, keep in mind that they sweeten as well as flavor. If you are avoiding sugar, use the unsweetened extracts and concentrates described previously to flavor your espresso-milk drinks. For specific suggestions and recipes, see pages 143–144, 149–150.

Serving Receptacles and Other Accessories. Each of the traditional espresso drinks has a preferred serving receptacle. They are specified in the descriptions of the various drinks.

In Italy, espresso is almost never dispensed into Styrofoam or cardboard. Such materials kill the delicate perfume of straight espresso. Rather than carrying their coffee back to work with them, Italians usually down a quick one standing at the bar, then fire off to work from there. This habit reflects the "small, powerful, perfect" aesthetic of Italian espresso cuisine.

One does see elegantly clad waiters and gofers hurrying through the business districts of large Italian cities carrying espresso drinks on trays, but these drinks are almost always dispensed into lovely insulated cups provided by the businessperson who is about to receive the coffee from his or her favorite bar. These little covered, insulated cups are usually made of metal and are refined expressions of the designer's art. The larger, insulated "to go" cups made of plastic and sold in many North American specialty coffee stores are as practical and ecologically sound as their Italian counterparts, but in aesthetic terms range from plain to ugly by comparison.

Classic, heavy demitasse and cappuccino cups and matching saucers, together with the tall, 16-ounce glasses used in most North American caffès for caffè latte, can be found at near-wholesale prices in restaurant supply stores. Such places also carry inexpensive demitasse spoons and long "iced tea" spoons to match the tall caffè latte glasses. More expensive, more distinctive, and often more fragile versions of these specialized receptacles and utensils are sold in kitchenware and specialty coffee stores. Some coffee stores also may carry glass or ceramic bowls reminiscent of those used to serve caffè latte in Italian-American caffès during earlier decades.

Small- to medium-sized stainless steel pitchers appropriate for frothing milk can be purchased in most North American specialty coffee stores. If you buy such a pitcher, make certain that it fits easily under the steam wand of your espresso brewer. A good frothing pitcher is light in weight, open at the top, with a broad pouring lip to facilitate coaxing frothed milk from pitcher to cup. These pitchers are quite useful, by the way, but not absolutely necessary. One can froth milk in a large ceramic mug.

Knockout boxes like those used by small restaurants and caffès to knock the spent grounds out of the filter in preparation for the next dose of coffee may be useful for those who entertain a good deal or who want to professionalize their espresso habit. A waste container with a solid edge works just as well, but isn't as spiffy.

Frothed milk thermometers assist in monitoring the exact heat of the milk under the froth, and help the novice avoid overheating the milk. I discuss these devices in more detail on pages 136–137.

If you have difficulty finding any of the accessories noted in this section, consult Finding Espresso Coffee and Equipment, pages 169–170.

(continued on page 130)

BREWING THE COFFEE

If the coffee is ground too coarsely or packed too loosely, the brewed coffee will gush out in a pale torrent, **top.** *If ground too finely or packed too tightly, it will ooze out in dark, reluctant drops,* **center.** *If ground and packed correctly, it will issue out properly in a slow but steady dribble,* **bottom.**

Note: The instructions that follow are meant to elaborate and complement those provided by the manufacturer of your espresso brewer. Be certain you have read and understood the safeguards, cautions, and instructions that accompany your brewing device before supplementing them with the advice and encouragement given below.

Coffee and Roast. Classic espresso is brewed using a coffee roasted dark brown, but not black. This roast usually is called *espresso* or *Italian* in stores. As long as the beans are properly ground you can use any coffee in your espresso brewer, but only with the classic espresso roast will you achieve the sweet, rich tang of the caffè drinks. See Chapter 6 for more on choosing coffee for espresso brewing.

Always use at least as much coffee as is recommended by the manufacturer of your machine. Never use less. The usual measure for commercial machines is a little less than 2 level tablespoons per serving. If in doubt, use 2 level tablespoons of finely ground coffee for every serving of espresso; in order to achieve a flavorful cup, you may have to use more. I find that with many home machines a single serving of espresso with the proper richness can be obtained only by using the double filter basket rather than the single, and by loading it with a double dose of ground coffee.

Brewing Principles. There are two requirements for making good espresso. First, you need to grind the coffee just fine enough and tamp it down in the filter basket just firmly and uniformly enough, so that the barrier of ground coffee resists the pressure of the hot water sufficiently to produce a slow dribble of either dark, rich liquid or golden crema. Second, you need to stop the dribble at just the right moment, before the oils in the coffee are exhausted and the dark, rich (or golden) dribble turns into a tasteless whitish-brown/brown torrent. See the illustration on the left.

Grind. The best grind for espresso is very fine and gritty but not a dusty powder. If you look at the ground coffee from a foot away, you should barely be able to distinguish the particles. If you rub some between your fingers, it should feel gritty. If you have whole beans ground at a store, ask for a fine grind for an espresso machine. A fine, precise, uniform grind is particularly important for pump and piston machines, which demand an especially dense layer of coffee to resist their high brewing pressure. See Chapter 7 for more on grind and grinders for espresso brewing.

Preheating Group, Filter Holder, and Cup. Servings of straight espresso are so small and delicate that everything immediately surrounding the brewing act must be warmed in advance to preserve heat in the freshly pressed coffee. If you have a pump or piston machine and are making your first cup, be sure to preheat the group, filter, and filter holder by running a small amount of hot brewing water through them. The demitasse into which you press the coffee should also be warm. Use the cup warmer on your machine, the top of your machine as an improvised cup warmer, or run some steam from the frothing wand into the cup. Those who drink their espresso with frothed milk can afford some carelessness in this regard; the hot milk usually manages to compensate for lukewarm coffee and a cool cup.

Filling and Tamping. Different types of brewing devices have somewhat differing requirements for this important operation.

A

For machines with external, caffè-style clamp-in filter and filter holder: Fill the filter basket with coffee to the point indicated by the manufacturer, distributing it evenly in the filter basket (A). Then press the coffee down, exerting roughly similar pressure across the entire surface of the dose. *With machines that work by steam pressure alone* use your fingertips to consistently but *lightly* press the coffee across its entire surface (B); don't hammer on it. *With pump and piston machines* use the device called a *tamper* that was packaged with your machine, and exert strong pressure, decisively

B

packing the coffee into the filter basket (C). As you tamp the coffee you might simultaneously twist the tamper, which *polishes* the surface of the coffee and assists in creating a uniform resistance to the brewing water.

Never use less than the minimum volume of ground coffee recommended for the machine, even if you are brewing a single cup. If the coffee gushes out rather than dribbling, compensate by using a finer grind or by tamping the coffee more firmly. If it still gushes out, use a bit more coffee and recheck the fineness of the grind. If it oozes out rather than dribbling steadily, use a coarser grind or go easier on the tamping.

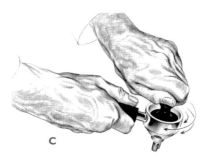

C

A note on self-tamping machines and pods and capsules: Some pump machines have a self-tamping feature; the shower head on the underside of the group automatically compresses the coffee as you clamp the filter holder into the machine. You still need to use the tamper to assure that the coffee is evenly distributed in the filter basket, however. Machines that brew with espresso pods or capsules require no tamping. The pods or capsules are simply inserted into the special filter holder. With these machines you still must time the brewing accurately, however (see below), to avoid ruining the espresso by running too much water through the ground coffee.

For stovetop espresso brewers with internal filter baskets (most brewers in categories 1 and 2, pages 108–109): Most stovetop espresso brewers contain the ground coffee in a largish sleeve inside the machine, rather than in a caffè-style filter unit that clamps to the outside of the machine. When using these stovetop devices with interior filter baskets, *do not tamp the coffee* unless the instructions for your machine ask you to do so. Use the same fine grind as recommended above, use as much as the manufacturer's instructions recommend, distribute it evenly in the filter basket, and proceed. For stovetop machines with caffè-style filter holders that clamp to the outside of the machine, tamp lightly as described above.

Clamping the Filter Holder into the Group: Always wipe off any grains of coffee that may have clung to the edges of the filter holder, since they may cause brewing water to leak around the edges of the filter and dilute the coffee. Also make certain that the filter holder is firmly and evenly locked into the group. Until you get the knack of the clamping gesture, you may need to stoop over and peer under the group to make certain that the filter holder is evenly snugged in place.

Brewing. Timing is everything in espresso brewing. The richest and most flavorful coffee issues out right at the beginning; as brewing continues, the coffee becomes progressively thinner and more bitter. Consequently, *collect only as much coffee as you will actually serve.* If you are brewing one serving, cut off the flow of coffee after one serving has dribbled out, even if you have two servings' worth of ground coffee in the filter basket. If you are brewing two servings, cut off the flow after two. And no matter how many servings you are trying to make, *never allow the coffee to bubble and* *gush into your serving carafe or cup*. Such thin, overextracted coffee will taste so bad that it's better to start over than to insult your palate or guests by serving it.

Gauge when to cut off the flow of coffee by sight, not by clock or timer. The fineness of the grind may vary, as will the pressure you apply when tamping. Consequently, the speed with which the hot water dribbles through the coffee will also vary from serving to serving. If in doubt, cut off the flow of coffee sooner rather than later. Better to experience a perfectly flavored small drink than an obnoxiously bitter large one. As you gauge the flow of coffee, keep in mind that it will continue to run into the cup or receptacle for a moment or two after you have turned off the pump or shut off the coffee valve.

If you have a pump machine, make certain not to leave the freshly brewed coffee under the group while you froth milk or busy yourself elsewhere. Most pump machines drip heavily, and you will return to find your coffee badly diluted.

Knock-Out and Cleaning. Pump and piston machines can be recharged with further doses of coffee while the machines are still hot. To remove spent grounds from a hot filter, turn the filter holder upside down and rap it smartly against the side of a sturdy waste container or against the cross-piece of the waste drawer that may have come with your system. This can be one of those pleasantly nonchalant gestures that perfects itself with time and practice. Wipe any leftover grounds off the edge of the filter holder and fill with the next dose of ground coffee. The true aficionado may wish to purchase a knock-out box of the kind used in small caffès. See page 125. A few machines may not incorporate a catch to retain the filter inside the filter holder; in this case you have no recourse but to dig out the grounds with a spoon.

Regularly wipe off the gasket and shower head on the underside of the group, where spent coffee grains tend to cling. Less often, pop the filter basket out of the filter holder and wash both parts. Take note of the manufacturer's instructions for decalcification. If you live in an area with particularly hard water, I would recommend using bottled water, particularly if you own a pump machine. The workings of these devices are particularly vulnerable to calcium build-up.

THE TRADITIONAL CUISINE AT HOME

Straight Espresso

If you wish to achieve the perfection of straight espresso at home, you need to purchase a small pump or manual lever machine (categories 4 or 5, pages 111–114). The brewing devices that work by steam pressure alone (categories 2 and 3, pages 109–110) will make good espresso drinks with milk but at best will produce a flavorful but thin-bodied imitation of the unadorned drink. A perfectly pressed espresso exits the filter holder in majestic deliberation, all heavy golden froth that only gradually condenses into a dark, rich liquid as it gathers in the cup. Such results can be gotten only with good technique on machines that exert more than the relatively feeble 1½ to 3 atmospheres of pressure generated by the steam-only devices in categories 1 through 3.

Once you have mastered the brewing routine (see pages 126–129), the next step in making straight espresso the way you like it is to experiment with blend and roast (see Chapter 6). If your espresso tastes too sharp, try lighter-roasted blends until you find one that suits you.

Sweeteners and Alternatives. Don't feel reluctant for reasons of sophistication to add sugar to straight espresso, by the way; Italians almost universally sweeten espresso, and the prejudice against adding sugar to coffee is one of those Puritan tics peculiar to North American culture. Honey, by the way, tends to die when added to coffee. Those who wish some nutrition with their sweetener might find raw or Demerara sugar a more effective and flavorful choice than honey for sweetening coffee drinks. If you don't care to sweeten your espresso for dietary reasons, then either experiment with drinks that add hot frothed milk to the espresso, which mellows the sharpness; or try a drop or two of one of the unsweetened flavorings I mentioned earlier: vanilla extract, almond extract, or one of the liquid concentrates designed to be added to coffee after brewing. These substances contribute a sweetish sensation to espresso without the use of sugar.

Crema. Crema, the golden froth that mists over the surface of a well-made straight espresso and the subject of mystical rhapsodies by Italian espresso lovers, can be a problem in home brewing. More specifically, its absence can be a problem. You can consistently achieve it only with the pump and piston machines in categories 4 and 5, pages 111–114. If you own such a machine, and brew carefully, following the suggestions on pages 126–129, your espresso should display the rich flavor and heavy body of the true product, together with at least some crema. If your espresso tastes good but you're not getting enough crema to make you happy, consult the relevant Espresso Break, pages 132–134, for some advice.

Receptacles. Straight espresso is traditionally served in a 3-ounce cup (demitasse or tazzina), with appropriately proportioned spoon and saucer. The tazzina must be warm when the coffee is pressed into it, or the heavy cup will excessively cool the delicate coffee.

Straight Espresso Variations. The normal serving size for a true, aficionado's espresso is about one half the volume of a 3-ounce demitasse, or 1½ ounces. *Corto, short,* or *short pull* means an espresso cut short at about

1 ounce. *Lungo*, *long*, or *long pull* refers to an espresso that almost completely fills the 3-ounce demitasse. In both cases, the amount of ground coffee filling the filter basket should be the same; i.e., one dose, or about 2 level tablespoons. The difference is the amount of water allowed to run through the coffee.

Espresso Romano is a normal serving of espresso with a twist of lemon on the side; a drop or two of juice from the peel is squeezed into the espresso before drinking it. Variations replace the lemon peel with orange or tangerine peel.

Doppio or double espresso is simply two servings of espresso, brewed with two servings' worth of ground coffee. The doppio, properly made, should fill only one half to two thirds of a 6-ounce cup with rich, creamy espresso. The suicidal *triple espresso* is simply a nearly full 6-ounce cup of espresso made with three servings worth of ground coffee. Since most home machines do not provide triple-size filter baskets, those fools who might be tempted to drink a triple need to make it at home with two separate pulls, or pressings.

For the *Americano*, essentially a North American style, filter-strength coffee made by diluting a serving of espresso with several ounces of hot water, see page 46.

Simple Drinks with Frothed Milk

The distinctions among the various classic caffè drinks involving coffee and hot milk described on pages 43–44—cappuccino, latte macchiato, caffè latte, etc.—may seem a bit arbitrary. After all, the only actual differences are simple: the proportion of espresso to milk, how the milk and coffee are combined, and the kind of receptacle one uses.

However, I can vouch for the fact that these seemingly insignificant differences in procedure and presentation make for rather dramatic differences in taste among the various traditional drinks. So even though the distinctions among the various espresso-milk drinks may blur when you are making them at home, it is well to understand the gustatory goals behind these differences.

Here is a summary of the traditional coffee-milk drinks:
Espresso Macchiato (espresso "marked," *macchiato*, with frothed milk). Adds just the slightest topping of hot frothed milk to a tazzina of espresso. Here the espresso comes through in its full-bodied, pungent completeness; the milk barely mellows the bite of the coffee. An excellent way to take espresso for those who avoid sugar but want the power of unadorned espresso. Good also after dinner, when a milkier drink like a cappuccino tastes too diffused and looks unsophisticated. Like straight espresso, served in a preheated 3-ounce demitasse.

Cappuccino. This is the prince (or princess) of espresso drinks made with milk. It is traditionally served in a 6-ounce cup, and the frothed milk is *added to the coffee in the cup*. The emphasis is on the froth rather than on the milk. A proper cappuccino is made with more milk than an espresso macchiato, but less than a latte macchiato, and considerably less than a caffè latte.

If a cappuccino is made correctly, the perfume and body of the espresso completely permeate the froth and

(continued on page 140)

THE CREMA QUESTION

Crema Connotations

Crema, the natural golden froth that graces the surface of a well-made tazzina of straight espresso, is an almost mystical obsession among Italian espresso lovers. Its only practical role is to help hold in some of the aroma until the coffee is drunk, but its cultural connotations are legion.

For Italian espresso professionals crema is the key to diagnosing the coffee underneath: Dark-colored crema indicates a blend heavy with robusta coffees; golden-colored crema reveals a blend based on higher-quality arabica coffees. Crema made up of a few, large bubbles indicates a coffee that has been brewed too quickly and is probably thin-bodied; dense, clotted crema indicates a coffee that has been brewed too slowly and may be burned. For the Italian bar operator crema is the mark of achievement: A perfect golden stream of froth descending majestically from the filter holder is a demonstration, endlessly repeated, of his mastery.

For those Italians who simply like good espresso, crema is a visual prelude to the sensual pleasure of the coffee itself, promising sweetness rather than bitterness, rounded richness rather than one-dimensional thinness.

Perhaps crema suggests even more. A tazzina of espresso without crema stares up at one with dark, disconcerting blankness, empty of promises, whereas a crema-covered cup seems veiled with intrigue and mystery. Crema intimates grace and elegance, abundance; by comparison a crema-less cup appears exposed and impoverished.

Crema and You

No doubt that last paragraph projects too much, but one cannot underestimate the role of crema in the mystique of straight espresso. The problem is, a cup of espresso *can* taste just as good without crema as with, and home espresso-lovers may find themselves so intimidated by the quest for crema that they may deny themselves the pleasure of enjoying an otherwise good tazzina of crema-less espresso.

So above all, if your espresso tastes good but has little crema, enjoy the coffee first and worry later about how it looks.

Given that heartfelt advice, here are a few steps to take if you continue to be tormented by crema-less espresso.

Steam-Pressure Brewer Caveat. If you are using a steam-pressure brewer (categories 1 through 3, pages 108–110), give up on crema or buy a pump or piston machine. If you follow the instructions for brewing on pages 126–129 very carefully, you may get a little crema at best from a steam-pressure brewer. These devices can make reasonably good espresso drinks with milk but will not produce a straight espresso with the richness and body, *or* the crema, of the caffè product.

Good Technique. If you are using a pump or piston machine (categories 4 and 5, pages 111–114), begin your pursuit of crema by reviewing your brewing technique against the instructions on pages 126–129. Make certain your grind is a fine grit, that you use sufficient coffee, that the coffee is evenly distributed in the filter, and that it has been tamped hard, with a twisting motion of the tamper to polish the surface of the dose.

Precision Grind. Above all, review the grind of your coffee. It should be a very fine grit, but also a uniform, flaked grit, produced either by a large, commercial grinder in a store or by a specialized home espresso grinder. See Chapter 7 for more on precision grind and how to get it.

Fresh Coffee. Make certain your coffee is fresh. If you buy whole-bean coffee in bulk, buy it from a vendor who emphasizes freshness, keep it in a sealed container in a cool dry place, and grind it as close to the moment of brewing as possible. If you use preground, canned coffee, buy it in smaller, half-sized cans; open the can just before brewing; and immediately transfer the excess coffee to a sealed container for storage.

Lots of Coffee. This may qualify as cheating, but often the only way to achieve good crema on some pump machines is by using more than the recommended amount of coffee per serving. The normal recommended dose of ground coffee per serving of espresso is a little less than two level tablespoons. For better crema use the double filter basket rather than the single and use at least half-again as much coffee per serving, or about three level tablespoons.

Small, Pre-Warmed Cup. Brew directly into a 3-ounce cup that has been *pre-warmed*. The warm, narrow cup will help build up and hold the crema.

Special Devices to Promote Crema. Some pump machines have special gadgets built into the filter holder to promote the formation of crema. All of those that I've tried help considerably. Unfortunately, one has to buy the entire machine to get the gadget, so this solution is appropriate only for those so infatuated by crema that they are willing to purchase a new machine to get it.

Turn Buddhist. Decide that plainness and substance are more important than a little illusory froth anyhow.

FROTHING THE MILK

Most Americans prefer espresso blended with hot, frothed milk in drinks like cappuccino or caffè latte. Fortunately, the majority of espresso-brewing appliances now sold in the United States have built-in steam apparatus for frothing milk. If you like espresso drinks with milk, make certain that any brewing device you purchase has such a mechanism. Look for a small pipe, usually about ¼ inch in diameter and a few inches long, protruding from the side or front of the device.

Heating milk with such apparatus is easy; producing a head of froth or foam is a little trickier but, like riding a bicycle or centering clay on a potter's wheel, exquisitely simple once you've broken through and gotten the hang of it.

Getting Started

There are three stages to making an espresso drink with frothed milk. The first is brewing the coffee; the second is frothing and heating the milk; the third is combining the two. Never froth the coffee and milk together, which would stale the fresh coffee and ruin the eye-pleasing contrast between white foam and dark coffee. Nor is it a good idea, even if your machine permits it, to simultaneously brew espresso and froth the milk. Concentrate on the brewing operation first, taking care to produce only as much coffee as you need. Then stop the brewing and turn to the frothing operation.

The Frothing Apparatus. See the illustration below. The steam wand, also called *steam stylus, pipe,* or *nozzle,* is a little tube that protrudes from the top or side of the machine (A). At the tip of the wand are one to four little holes that project jets of steam downward or diagonally when the steam function is activated, or in some cases a special nozzle designed to facilitate the frothing operation. Nearby you will find the knob that controls the flow of steam (B). While you are brewing coffee, this knob and the valve it controls are kept screwed shut.

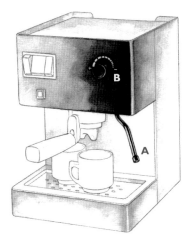

Some machines do not have a screw knob to control the flow of steam for frothing; instead, you simply activate the steam function with a switch, automatically releasing what the manufacturer considers to be the optimal flow of steam for the frothing operation.

Still other machines come with aerating nozzles on the end of the steam wand designed to make the frothing operation easier. These devices suck

*Three aerating nozzles designed to make milk-frothing easier. The removable Krups Perfect Froth device, **top**; the Braun Turbo Cappuccino, which incorporates a little spinning, fan-like element inside the nozzle, **center**; and the Saeco Cappuccino, **bottom**. The majority of espresso brewing devices sold in North America now incorporate such nozzles.*

additional room-temperature air into the milk along with the steam, presumably helping to fluff up the milk. Most still require a conventional frothing technique as described below. They do not replace the traditional frothing procedure; they simply make it easier. However, one aerating nozzle, the Krups Perfect Froth, requires a completely different technique, described in the Krups literature. With virtually any other kind of steam nozzle or apparatus you will find the following instructions helpful, if not essential.

Do not feel deprived if your machine has a conventional frothing apparatus, by the way. Anyone with the smallest amount of patience can master the normal frothing operation and in the process gain considerably more control over the texture and dimension of the froth than is possible with the less conventional apparatus. And frothing milk the old-fashioned way may turn out to be one of those noble, Zen-like rituals that stubbornly resist progress, like manual shifting in sports cars, wooden bats in baseball, and catching fish with dry flies.

The Milk. Virtually any liquid dairy product, from skimmed milk to heavy cream, as well as most imitation liquid dairy products such as soy milk, can be frothed using the steam apparatus of an espresso brewing device. More on choosing milk for espresso drinks is given on page 122. For beginners milk with more butterfat may be slightly easier to froth than milk with less. I suggest you begin with ordinary whole milk.

Frothing Pitchers and Milk Thermometers. Milk can be frothed in any relatively wide-mouthed container that fits under the steam wand of your machine. If you're a caffè latte drinker you can simply froth the milk in the same mug or heat-resistant glass you use to assemble and consume your drink. However, small stainless-steel pitchers designed specifically for milk frothing are useful. They are light in weight and usually have a broad, rolled pouring lip, which facilitates moving the froth and milk together in one smooth motion from pitcher to cup.

Milk frothing thermometers resemble meat thermometers and clip on the edge of the frothing pitcher, with the dial facing up and the temperature probe extending into the pitcher. These thermometers assist in monitoring the exact heat of the milk under the froth (135° F if you plan to enjoy your drink immediately, up to 165° F if there will be a delay in serving or drinking it), and help the novice avoid one of the most prevalent errors of milk frothing: overheating or scalding the milk. However, I find that simply feeling the side of the milk frothing container (when it's too hot to touch, stop frothing) works just as well.

Transition Between Brewing and Frothing. In less expensive, steam-pressure machines (categories 2 and 3, pages 109–110) and in piston machines (category 5, pages 113–114) this transition is accomplished simply by closing the coffee-brewing valve or ending the coffee-brewing operation and opening the steam valve. In button-operated pump machines (category 4, pages 111–112), there is usually a more complex transitional procedure, which will be described in the instructions accompanying your machine. The transition involves raising the temperature of the boiler where the water is heated from the somewhat lower temperature best for brewing to a higher temperature suitable for producing steam. You press a button and wait twenty or thirty seconds for the boiler to achieve the higher temperature. In such machines it is *particularly important to bleed the hot water from the steam pipe before beginning to froth milk*, since a substantial residue of water usually collects in the pipe during brewing. Place an empty frothing pitcher or cup under the steam wand and open the valve. Wait until all of the hot water has sputtered out of the pipe and a steady hiss of steam is escaping from the nozzle before beginning the frothing operation.

A Dry Run. Before attempting to froth milk for the first time, practice opening and closing the steam valve with the machine on, the brewing function off or closed, and the steam function activated. Get a general sense of how many turns it takes to create an explosive jet of steam and how many to permit a steady, powerful jet. It is the latter intensity that you will use to froth milk: not so powerful that the jet produces an overpowering roar but powerful enough to produce a strong, steady hiss.

If you are using a stovetop machine and the steam is not producing a sturdy hiss, raise the heat slightly and make certain that pressure is not escaping through the coffee valve. If steam explodes out of the wand at the first half-turn of the knob, reduce the heat under the machine. You should be able to open the knob at least a quarter- to a half-turn before the full force of the steam is heard and felt.

The Frothing Routine

You can froth the milk in a separate pitcher, or, if you are not a purist, in each cup or glass before you add the coffee. Small pitchers appropriate for frothing milk are sold in most coffee specialty stores. If you buy one, make certain that it will fit easily under the steam wand of your machine. In either case:

A

- Fill the container or cup *no more than halfway* with cold milk (the colder the better; hot milk will not produce froth).

- Open the steam valve for a few seconds to bleed any hot water from inside the wand into an empty cup or container. Then close the valve until just a tiny bit of steam is escaping from the tip of the wand. This is to prevent milk from being sucked back up into the wand as you immerse it into the milk.

- Holding the container vertically, immerse the tip of the wand deeply into the milk (A). Slowly open the valve, then gradually close it until you get a strong, but not explosive, release of steam that moves the surface of the milk, but doesn't wildly churn it.

B

- Now slowly lower the milk container, thus bringing the tip of the wand closer to the surface of the milk (B). When the wand tip is just below the surface of the milk, you will hear a rough-edged hissing sound, the surface will begin to seethe, and frothy bubbles will begin to form. If the wand tip is too deep in the milk, there will be no hiss and the surface will not seethe; if it is too shallow, you will spray milk all over your apron. If it is just right, a gratifying head of froth will begin to rise from the surface of the milk. You need to follow the froth upward as it develops. Listen for the hiss; if you don't hear it, or if it turns to a dull rumble, the wand is too deep in the milk.

C

- The first swelling of froth will be made up of largish, unstable bubbles. Periodically drop the tip of the steam wand back into the milk and hold it there for a moment, to let some of these bubbles pop and settle. Then bring the tip of the wand back to just below the surface of the milk again to rebuild the head of froth. Repeat this process until you have a creamy, dense head of froth made up of a stable matrix of tiny bubbles.

Heating the Milk. At this point, feel the sides of the milk container to see when the milk is hot. If it is not, lower the wand tip completely into the milk and keep it there until the sides of the container are just a little too hot to be touched comfortably (C). If you are using a milk thermometer (see page 136), stop heating when the milk reaches a temperature between 135° F and 165° F, the latter if there will be a delay in serving or drinking. Never heat the milk to boiling, and again, always froth the milk first, before you heat it, since cold milk froths best. If you are frothing milk for the first time and you end up with hot milk and not much froth, enjoy what you have and try again later with cold milk.

Finishing the Frothing Operation. Always conclude by opening the steam valve for a few seconds to clear milk residues from the nozzle. If you are using an inexpensive machine that utilizes simple steam pressure to force the water through the coffee, it is a good idea to let the steam valve remain open after you turn off the machine, to bleed the remaining steam from the boiler and relieve pressure on the valves and gaskets. The simpler steam apparatus require wiping only with a damp cloth; some of the more complex aerating frothing nozzles need to be periodically disassembled and the parts thoroughly cleaned. Occasionally milk residues may completely clog the tiny holes through which the steam issues, in which case you will need to poke them open with a needle. Perform this operation *with the steam valve closed*, to avoid a sudden blast of hot steam.

If you don't immediately raise an impressive head of froth, be patient. You may have to suffer through a few naked cappuccini at first, but inside a week you'll be frothing like a Milanese master.

Other Uses for the Steam Function. The steam wand also can be used to heat hot chocolate concentrate for various espresso-chocolate drinks (see page 142), and to preheat cups and glasses. In most pump machines the steam wand also will deliver hot water for tea and other beverages; see the instructions that come with your machine.

oughout the drink without losing a
er, while the sharpness of the coffee is
ut being subdued. By comparison, the
orth American "latte" is milky, feeble, and
insipid.

However, few are the cappuccinos that are made
correctly. Italian espresso blends are made to be drunk
straight, so the Italian cappuccino is usually bland. On the
other hand, the North American cappuccino is typically
bitter. The beans have been overroasted, the coffee
overextracted, and the milk has been frothed too stiffly,
so that it floats to the top of the espresso rather than
subtly uniting with it.

Even made incorrectly, the cappuccino is a pleasant
drink. But made correctly, it is an experience that turns
ordinary coffee drinkers into obsessives, searching the
world, or at least their neighborhoods, for a good cappuccino, and even reading entire books like this one to
find the secret of how to assemble one at home.

Secrets of the Cappuccino. Here is how to assemble
an authentic cappuccino at home:

- Make a perfectly pressed, very rich, *small* quantity
  of espresso, 1 to 2 ounces, no more. Use a pump
  or piston machine if possible, and follow the
  instructions for pressing coffee on pages 126–129
  as precisely as possible. Use a good North
  American espresso blend, dark brown, with oil just
  beginning to appear on the surface of the bean.
  Press the coffee into a warm 6-ounce cup.

- Froth the milk to the point that it is still dense and a
  bit soupy, full of many tiny bubbles rather than a

relatively few large ones. It should *barely* peak if you
move a spoon through it. It should *not* stand up
puffily. It should be hot, but not scalding. See pages
135–139 for instructions on frothing milk.

- Pour the frothed milk into the cup. If you have
  frothed the milk correctly and if you are using a thin-
  edged metal pitcher, the milk and froth should move
  together into the cup. You may need to encourage
  the froth with a spoon, however. The milk should
  not (cannot if it is frothed correctly) stand up like
  meringue above the top edge of the cup. An indication that you have done everything perfectly is a
  brilliant white oval or heart shape on the surface of
  the drink, surrounded on all sides by a ring of dark
  brown, created by the espresso crema that has
  been carried to the surface of the milk.

Obviously, such precision does not come with your
first home cappuccino; but if you have some idea what
you are trying to achieve, your very first attempts should
taste better than the production of most North American caffès.

Latte Macchiato. Milk "marked" or "stained" with
espresso; the opposite of *espresso macchiato*, in which the
milk marks the espresso rather than espresso marking the
milk. There is not a great difference between espresso
macchiato and caffè latte. Made at home, the two drinks
certainly will tend to overlap. With the latte macchiato the
espresso is poured into a medium-sized glass of hot milk.
The emphasis is on the milk, not the foam, and the coffee,
when dribbled into the glass, usually stains the milk in
gradations, all contrasting with the modest white head of

froth. The latte macchiato is a breakfast or early-day drink; it is the Italian version of the North American caffè latte.

Obviously the better and richer the espresso, the better the latte macchiato, but *crema* is irrelevant, and you can get away with espresso that is flavorful but somewhat light-bodied, the kind you can achieve with the modest steam-pressure machines of categories 2 and 3, pages 109–110. The sharp-flavored, oily, very dark roasts preferred by many North American caffès and roasters come into their own in the latte macchiato and caffè latte; the sharp flavor penetrates the milk better than the more rounded, sweeter roasts and blends that are appropriate for straight espresso.

The classic macchiato is made with 1 to 2 ounces of well-brewed espresso, dribbled into about 5 ounces or so of hot milk, topped with froth in an 8-ounce glass. But the exact proportions hardly matter; the essential idea is hot milk, coffee, a little froth, and a tallish glass.

Caffè Latte. The caffè latte dilutes the espresso in even more milk, in a taller glass or a bowl, with the espresso and milk poured simultaneously into the glass or bowl. The "latte" is definitely a breakfast drink. The original idea was to provide something to dip your breakfast roll into and enough liquid to wash the roll down with afterwards. As with the latte macchiato, the head of froth is usually modest, so as not to interfere with the roll-dipping operation and not to distract from the psychological sensation of virtually bathing in hot, milky liquid.

The North American "latte" usually combines one serving (1½ to 2 ounces) of espresso with enough milk to fill a 12- to 16-ounce glass. This recipe produces a weak, milky drink and has encouraged various customizations involving less milk and more espresso. In Seattle, for example, a terminology has evolved that permits the espresso bar customer to specify both number of servings of espresso (*single*, *double*, or *triple*) and volume of milk (*small*, or enough milk to fill an 8-ounce container; *tall*, enough to fill a 12-ounce container; or *mondo*, enough to fill 16 ounces). Thus a latte can range from a powerful drink with three servings of espresso and only a few ounces of milk to a drink in which a single serving of espresso barely flavors a virtual kindergarten class's worth of hot milk.

Obviously all of this terminology has little application to assembling a caffè latte at home. You experiment with the proportions of milk to coffee until you arrive at a satisfying balance. Most people customize the proportions to suit the moment: They may crave a stronger or a weaker drink, depending on the time of day and the current state of their nervous systems and work schedules.

The standard receptacle in the United States for the caffè latte is the plain, 16-ounce tapered restaurant glass used in other contexts for serving everything from milk shakes to beer. A more interesting and arguably more authentic serving receptacle for the caffè latte is a relatively deep 12- to 16-ounce ceramic or glass bowl.

The Traditional Caffè Mocha

Next to the cappuccino, the caffè Mocha is probably the most abused drink in the traditional espresso cuisine. The classic Italian-American caffè Mocha combines a serving

(1 to 2 ounces) of espresso and perhaps 2 ounces of *strong*, usually *unsweetened* hot chocolate in a tallish 6- to 8-ounce ceramic mug, topped with hot milk and froth. The drink is sweetened to taste after it has been assembled and served, just as with any other espresso beverage. This drink, smoothly perfumy and powerful, has been turned into a sort of hot milkshake by many North American caffès. Operators essentially make a caffè latte, then pour a dollop of chocolate fountain syrup into it. With a true Mocha the chocolate flavor is true, deep, and strong; it permeates the froth and roars down your throat, playing a sort of tantalizing tag with the taste of the equally powerful espresso.

Those who wish to enjoy a home version of the counterfeit caffè Mocha have only to buy a good chocolate fountain syrup and add it to taste to a caffè latte or cappuccino. Those who are interested in experimenting with the classic caffè Mocha will need to make a chocolate concentrate. One part unsweetened, dark chocolate powder mixed with two parts hot water or milk makes an authentic version of this concentrate. The powder and water or milk can be combined while heating them with the steam wand of the espresso machine. As you direct the steam into the water and chocolate, stir with a spoon or small whisk, working the floating clumps of dry chocolate down into the gradually heating water or milk. Either sweeten the mixture to taste when you mix it (try brown or Demerara sugar), or leave it unsweetened, giving you and your guests an opportunity to sweeten the assembled drink after it has been served. If you prefer a lighter-tasting concentrate, add a few drops

of vanilla extract to the mix while you are heating it. Try about 1/4 teaspoon to every cup of chocolate powder, adjusting to taste.

To make the classic caffè Mocha, combine about 2 ounces of this concentrate with one serving (1 1/2 to 2 ounces) of espresso and enough hot, frothed milk to fill a 6- to 8-ounce mug. Vary the proportions of chocolate, espresso, milk, and froth to taste.

Once mixed, by the way, the chocolate concentrate can be stored in a capped jar in the refrigerator for up to three weeks, or if you've used milk, until the milk sours. The mixture may separate; when you are ready to use the concentrate, invert and shake the jar, then pour out into a frothing pitcher or mug as much concentrate as you wish to consume, and reheat it, using the steam wand.

Some caffès now use a white-chocolate concentrate to produce special espresso drinks with names like "White-Chocolate Mocha," "Bianco Mocha," etc. To make such a white-chocolate concentrate, melt in a double boiler approximately 2 ounces sweetened white baking chocolate in 1/2 cup boiling water. Bring the mixture to a boil, then reduce heat to a low bubbling boil for about 3 minutes, stirring regularly. This concentrate also can be refrigerated for up to three weeks. Substitute it for the chocolate concentrate in caffè Mocha and other chocolate-espresso-frothed milk drinks. It contributes a sweet, delicately flavored chocolate component.

Both of these chocolate concentrates can be used to make hot chocolate drinks without espresso; simply combine the concentrate to taste with hot frothed milk.

THE CONTEMPORARY AMERICAN CUISINE AT HOME

The contemporary American or Seattle cuisine brings an exuberant sense of experiment to espresso tradition. Most of its innovations can be duplicated easily at home.

Adding Flavors to Espresso at Home

The ingredients section leading off this chapter describes the various classes of flavorings in the new North American espresso cuisine. Making use of these flavorings at home could not be simpler: You simply add them in their appropriate form to your favorite drink.

Flavoring Straight Espresso. Try a few drops of one of the unsweetened, concentrated flavorings described on page 123; add the flavoring after the coffee is brewed. Or add 10 to 25 percent flavored whole beans to an espresso blend before grinding and brewing.

Flavoring Frothed Milk Drinks. Simply add Italian-style fountain syrup to taste. The widely available Torani line of syrups seems to offer a version of virtually every flavor known to Western culture. Competing lines of syrups present similar variety.

Here are some suggestions for specific drinks:

Flavored caffè latte. If you make your caffè latte in a 12-ounce glass, start with ½ to 1 ounce of syrup to one serving (1½ to 2 ounces) of espresso and about 8 ounces of hot frothed milk. You can either stir in the syrup after you have assembled the drink or mix the syrup into the milk as you froth it, in which case the syrup will faintly color the milk and froth. Nut flavors (orgeat/almond, hazelnut) and spice (vanilla, anisette, crème de menthe, chocolate mint) are good places to start.

Flavored cappuccino. Go very lightly with the syrup here, ¼ to ½ ounce at the most, or you may ruin the balance of the drink. Make a classic cappuccino (see pages 131, 140). Add the syrup after the cappuccino is assembled. If you enjoy visual drama, try moving your hand across the surface of the drink as you pour the syrup, causing it to stain the milk in an attractive diagonal pattern (or creatively messing up the counter).

Flavored caffè Mocha. Make a classic Mocha (see pages 141–142), then add a dash of hazelnut, almond, orange, or mint syrup.

For still further extravagances, see the section on Soda Fountain Espresso at Home: Hot Drinks (pages 144–149, 150), and Soda Fountain Espresso at Home: Cold Drinks (pages 150–151).

Garnishes. The traditional garnishes (unsweetened chocolate, cinnamon, grated nutmeg, and grated orange peel) are now augmented by an array of sweetened and unsweetened garnishing powders put out by various firms and marketed in fancy food and specialty coffee stores. See page 123. If you combine one flavor of syrup and another of garnish you have an opportunity to either subtly delight the palate or grossly confuse it. Flavor combinations that seem to marry well with espresso are orange and chocolate, almond and chocolate, hazelnut and chocolate, mint and chocolate, and orange and vanilla. Make the syrup one choice and the garnish the other.

Coffeeless Espresso Cuisine

So long as you have the machine, the garnishes, the milk and the syrups, you might consider some espresso cuisine without the espresso.

Flavored frothed milk. This drink appears in caffès under a variety of names, from the no-nonsense "Steamer" to the fanciful "Moo." Add syrup to taste to frothed milk (start with ½ to 1 ounce syrup per 8 ounces milk). Mix the syrup into the milk during frothing or after.

Hot chocolate, Cioccolata. Make a chocolate concentrate (see page 142), and top 3 to 4 ounces of hot concentrate with 4 to 5 ounces of hot frothed milk, to fill an 8-ounce mug. Garnish with chocolate powder, vanilla powder, grated orange peel, or shaved white chocolate.

Hot chocolate with whipped cream, Cioccolata con Panna. Halve the milk in the previous recipe and top with whipped cream, either unsweetened, sweetened, or flavored (for flavoring whipped cream see below).

Soda Fountain Espresso at Home: Hot Drinks

Once you have mastered the basic exclamatory vocabulary of syrups, frothed milk, espresso, and garnishes, you may want to add whipped cream to your repertoire. Add moderately stiff whipped cream (sweetened or unsweetened) to any espresso drink in place of a roughly similar volume of frothed milk. In other words, if you make a caffè Mocha, omit about 2 ounces of frothed milk and replace it with a healthy dollop of whipped cream to fill the mug. Garnish the whipped cream as you would the frothed milk.

The company that manufactures Torani syrups suggests flavored whipped cream. Blend 1 pint whipping cream with 3 to 4 ounces syrup. Store this sweetened, flavored whipped cream and use it as suggested above. Thus, if you're careful and don't get too dizzy with your choice of flavors, you can serve a flavored caffè latte topped with a second flavor of whipped cream. And, of course, a dash of garnish to the whipped cream will complicate the business still further.

Try, for example, orange-flavored whipped cream on a classic caffè Mocha or simply vanilla-flavored whipped cream on straight espresso, with a garnish of chocolate powder. I won't tempt the ghosts of espresso purists past with anything more complex than those rather modest suggestions; experiment. Maraschino whipped cream on a passion fruit-flavored cappuccino, garnished with orange peel? I can hear Signore Gaggia rolling around from here.

Caffè Americano

The Americano is another innovation apparently developed in Seattle; it permits the production of something resembling North American-style filter coffee on an espresso machine. The trick is to make a single 1- to 2-ounce serving of espresso, then *add hot water to taste*. If you simply run several ounces of hot water through a single dose of ground coffee, you will end up destroying the subtle aromatics of the espresso with the harsh-tasting chemicals that continue to be extracted from the coffee after it has given up its flavor oils. If, on the other hand, you make a 6-ounce cup of coffee with three doses

(continued on page 149)

Troubleshooting for Brewing and Frothing

Coffee Brewing

Machine is on, but no coffee appears.

- Coffee valve is not open, or brewing switch is not on.
- Steam valve is open, and pressure is escaping out steam wand.
- There is no water in boiler (for steam pressure and piston machines) or in reservoir (for pump machines). In pump machines, the removable reservoir may not be properly seated.
- Coffee is too finely ground, too powdery, or tamped too firmly. If coffee valve is open or brewing switch on and boiler or reservoir is full, and still no coffee appears, *immediately turn off power or heat*, wait until device cools, and reload with a somewhat coarser grind of coffee, tamped less firmly.
- Pump or other inner workings may be clogged with calcium deposits. Decalcify according to manufacturer's directions.

Coffee gushes out; tastes thin and bitter.

- Coffee grind is not fine enough; coffee has not been evenly distributed and tamped firmly in filter.
- Not enough coffee in filter.

Coffee oozes out slowly; tastes burned or baked.

- Coffee has been ground too finely and/or tamped too firmly. Coarsen grind, ease up on tamping, or use less coffee.

Coffee appears very watery; looks and tastes thin.

- Water may be escaping around edges of filter holder and dripping directly into cup without passing through coffee. Make certain filter holder is firmly and evenly snugged in place; make certain lumps of coffee grains have not interfered with seal around edges of filter holder. If machine is old, gasket on underside of group may be worn or compressed, permitting leakage. Check gasket and replace if necessary.

Coffee dribbles out properly but still tastes thin and bitter.

- Brew coffee according to instructions on pages 126–129. Do not allow excessive water to run through ground coffee. Brew only 1 to 1 1/2 ounces espresso per serving or dose of ground coffee.

Straight espresso tastes good but lacks crema.

- With steam-pressure machines: Significant crema is almost impossible to achieve with steam-pressure brewers. Occasionally some can be gotten by using large doses of fresh coffee and by meticulously following brewing instructions on pages 126–129.
- With pump or piston machines: Use fresh coffee; use plenty of it; make certain coffee is ground with precision on a large commercial grinder or a specialized home espresso grinder (see Chapter 7); tamp coffee firmly with twisting motion of tamper to polish surface of coffee; brew into a preheated, half-size cup (tazzina, demitasse) to compress and exaggerate crema. For more on crema production, see pages 132–134.

Coffee has good flavor but is thin and lacks body.

- With steam-pressure machines: Follow instructions for good espresso brewing, pages 126–129. Even at best, espresso brewed with steam-pressure machines will not be as rich and full-bodied as espresso produced by pump and piston machines.
- With pump or piston machines: Follow instructions for good espresso brewing, pages 126–129, with particular attention to fine, precision grind. Increase amount of ground coffee per serving.

Coffee has good body and richness but tastes too sharp.

- Coffee is probably too darkly roasted or too acidy for your taste. Choose a coffee somewhat lighter in roast than North American espresso norm, if possible one blended for Northern Italian tastes. In a pre-ground, canned espresso coffee look for one roasted and blended in Italy; in a straight, unblended coffee try dark-roasted Mexican Coatepec or Oaxaca, Peruvian, or Brazilian Santos.

Coffee has good body but tastes too bland. Flavor of coffee dies out in frothed-milk drinks.

- Coffee is probably too lightly roasted or too mild for your taste. Choose a coffee somewhat darker in roast, with an oily surface, blended for West Coast American tastes. In a pre-ground, canned coffee try a coffee roasted and blended for Latin tastes. In a straight, unblended coffee, try dark-roasted Kenyan, Colombian, or Guatemalan.

Coffee tastes good but is lukewarm.

- Preheat group, filter holder, and filter by running hot brewing water through them before beginning brewing operation. Brew directly into a preheated cup.

Milk Frothing

Frothing valve is open but no steam issues from nozzle.

- Frothing function may not be turned on.
- Steam valve is not open or not opened sufficiently.
- Nozzle openings may be clogged with milk residue. Close steam valve, turn off and cool down machine, and thoroughly clean nozzle, opening clogged holes with a needle.
- Boiler or water reservoir may be empty; in pump machines removable water reservoir may not be properly seated.

Steam issuing from nozzle is weak, even with valve fully open.

- If brewer is a stovetop model, raise heat.
- In a pump machine: Make certain steam function is activated and ready light is on. If you have frothed milk for more than one drink, you may have temporarily

exhausted steam supply in boiler; wait until ready light goes on again, then resume frothing.

- Clean nozzle and nozzle outlets.

After frothing, milk tastes weak and diluted.

- In a pump machine, make certain all hot water has been bled from steam pipe before beginning to froth. See page 137.

Milk still won't froth, even after all frothing directions on pages 135–139 were followed.

- Start with cold milk, not warm or hot. Froth milk first, then heat it. When frothing, make certain nozzle head is just below surface of milk, producing a bubbly, rough-edged hiss and causing surface of milk to seethe.
- Relax. It will come.

Espresso-and-frothed milk drinks taste watery; lack richness.

- Use whole milk rather than milk with reduced butterfat.
- Brew coffee according to instructions on pages 126–129. Do not allow excessive water to run through ground coffee. Brew only 1 to 1 1/2 ounces espresso per serving or dose of ground coffee.
- With a pump machine, make certain that you move the receptacle containing brewed coffee out from under the filter holder and group while you froth milk. Pump machines tend to drip during the frothing operation, sometimes diluting an otherwise well-brewed serving of espresso.
- Increase the amount of ground coffee per serving.

of coffee, you are simply delivering a triple espresso, rather than an Americano, which retains the perfumes of the original espresso while extending them with hot water into a longer drink.

For those who like the fresh aromatics of espresso but also crave the lightness and length of a North American-style filter coffee, the Americano, made correctly, is a good compromise. Medium-roasted varietal coffees as well as dark-roasted coffees can be brewed using the Americano method, and some Seattle-style caffès and carts do exactly that. They brew an Ethiopian Harrar Americano, a Sumatran Americano, etc.

Iced Espresso Drinks

You can make almost any espresso drink iced. There are several principles to be observed in converting hot drink recipes to cold, however:

- Use partly crushed ice or ice in smallish cubes, to achieve a thorough mutual penetration of ice and coffee.

- Use cold milk rather than hot milk in iced cappuccino, caffè latte, etc., so as not to melt the ice prematurely, thus overly diluting the coffee. If you wish to provide a decorative head of froth to dress up the drink and provide a setting for garnishes, add a modest topping of hot froth *after* you have combined the ice, coffee, and cold milk.

- Espresso that has been brewed and then refrigerated will not make as flavorful a drink as freshly brewed hot espresso, but holds its strength better when poured over the ice. Take your choice.

- The home-mixed chocolate concentrate I recommend for the hot caffè Mocha tends to separate in iced drinks. You may find a pre-mixed fountain syrup more satisfactory for a cold summer caffè Mocha.

The Traditional Espresso Granita. The classic Italian-American granita, more a dessert than a beverage, has become difficult to find in the United States, whereas partly frozen espresso-milk-sugar drinks dispensed from machines and sold under names like "latte granita" or "granita latte" are booming in popularity.

The classic granita consists of straight espresso that has been frozen and crushed, then served in a sundae dish and topped with whipped cream. When eating it, the powerful espresso ice and the whipped cream are combined in judiciously balanced spoonfuls.

For those who wish to experiment with this disappearing delicacy at home: Brew two doses of full-strength espresso per serving, freeze in an ice cube tray, then crush thoroughly before serving in a smallish parfait or sundae dish. Top with lightly sweetened whipped cream dusted with chocolate powder.

The "Latte Granita." The "latte granita" and similar partly frozen drinks sold at caffès and carts are dispensed from machines that maintain the espresso-milk-sugar mixture at freezing temperature while agitating it to prevent its solidifying. The result is a pleasantly grainy beverage: sweet, milky, and refreshing.

It is difficult to duplicate the heavy, grainy texture of the commercial latte granita at home, but home versions can be more flavorful because the espresso component is fresh, rather than several hours old. For each serving brew one serving (about 1½ to 2 ounces) of full-strength espresso. While the espresso is still hot, sweeten heavily to taste. (If in doubt, start with 3 rounded teaspoons of sugar to each serving.) Chill the sweetened espresso, then combine in a blender with about 2 ounces of cold milk and 3 ice cubes per serving, partly crushed. Blend very lightly, until the ice is barely pulverized and still grainy, and serve immediately. Experiment with the amount of milk, ice, espresso, and sweetener until you obtain a custom balance that satisfies you. You can brew the espresso in advance and store it in a capped jar in the refrigerator for convenience, although the longer you refrigerate it, the slightly less flavorful your "latte granita" will be.

Soda Fountain Espresso at Home: Cold Drinks

Espresso (sweetened to taste while hot), cold milk, ice, flavored syrups, garnishes, and ice cream can be combined in a literally endless number of ways. Here are just a few suggestions.

Affogato. Pour 1 or 2 servings of espresso over vanilla ice cream. Either stop there and start eating, or top with whipped cream (flavored or unflavored), and garnish with grated chocolate (white or dark), chocolate powder, or grated orange peel.

Cappuccino and Ice Cream. Combine a serving (1½ to 2 ounces) espresso with 4 ounces cold milk; lay in a scoop of vanilla, chocolate, or coffee ice cream. If you prefer, top with a dollop of whipped cream and a dash of garnish.

Espresso Fizz. Pour one serving (1½ to 2 ounces) espresso in a tall 12-ounce glass; add sugar to taste (try 1 teaspoon); fill with ice and soda water. Serve unmixed so that the drama of the espresso lurking at the bottom of the drink can be appreciated. Before drinking mix with an iced tea or soda spoon.

Espresso Egg Creme. Pour 1 ounce milk and 1 serving (1½ to 2 ounces) espresso in a tall 12-ounce glass; sweeten to taste; fill with ice and soda water; serve as in the previous recipe.

Mocha Egg Creme. Pour 1 ounce milk, 1 serving (1½ to 2 ounces) expresso, and 1 to 1½ ounces chocolate concentrate (see page 142) or commercial chocolate syrup in a tall 12-ounce glass; sweeten to taste unless the chocolate is already sweetened; fill glass with ice and soda water and serve as in the previous recipes.

Italian Soda. The syrups used in the contemporary American espresso cuisine were originally intended as soft drink syrups. Combine 1 to 1½ ounces of one of these Italian-style syrups with ice and soda water to fill a tall 12-ounce glass. If you haven't already, try orgeat (almond) or tamarindo (date).

Italian Egg Creme. Pour 1 ounce milk and 1 to 1½ ounces syrup in the bottom of a tall 12-ounce glass; fill with ice and soda water.

Espresso Float. Make an *Espresso Fizz* or *Espresso Egg Creme* with chilled soda water but without the ice; leave space at the top of a 12- or 16-ounce glass; add 1 or 2 scoops of any flavor ice cream.

Espresso Ice Cream Soda. Make an *Espresso Float* in a 16-ounce glass, leaving room at the top for whipped cream, flavored or unflavored, garnished with grated chocolate or orange peel.

You get the idea. Empty the freezer and carry on.

ESPRESSO SERVICE
AT HOME FOR THE 1990s

Since espresso cuisine in the 1990s has become so varied in its manifestations, and any group of guests is likely to include a mix of purists, Seattle-style post-modernists, and espresso innocents, those readers who entertain in conventional fashion may wish to serve their espresso cuisine buffet-style and allow their guests to doctor their espresso themselves. The garnishes, unsweetened flavorings, and Italian syrups described earlier in this chapter all have a long shelf life. The syrups in particular are attractively packaged and look colorful arrayed on a tray or buffet.

The do-it-yourself approach also can be extended to assembling the traditional milk and espresso drinks. Serve a largish pitcher of hot, frothed milk; a smaller pitcher of fresh espresso; and perhaps a pitcher of freshly mixed Italian-style hot chocolate, unsweetened, with sugar on the side; and let your guests have their way with it all.

Purists, of course, will justifiably want their demitasse of espresso or their cappuccino brewed into the cup and served fresh, but those latte lovers who order a double mint mocha or whatever will doubtless be happier wading in themselves.

ESPRESSO DRINKS
FORTIFIED WITH SPIRITS

Although there are many traditional recipes that combine spirits with drip or filter coffee, by comparison there is little precedent for drinks that marry espresso with alcohol. Perhaps the concentrated nature of espresso discourages such experiments. With the addition of flavored caffè lattes and "latte granitas" to the cuisine, North American espresso culture seems to be drifting more toward association with the soda fountain than with the saloon. This trend may be owing partly to coffee's (and tea's) privileged position as the only widely consumed intoxicants that have so far made it through the gauntlet of modern medical testing without having been definitely implicated in any diseases. Perhaps by dissociating espresso from hard liquor, today's coffee culture is attempting to consolidate coffee's position as the "nice vice" of the 1990s.

Nevertheless, those adults whose vices are still nice but more wide-ranging will find that many spirits and liqueurs used with gustatory discretion make an attractive complement to espresso.

Any espresso drink can be lightly fortified with brandy, which complicates both the flavor and effect of the drink without overwhelming its essential nature. Dark rum, grappa, anise-flavored spirits like Pernot and ouzo, and bourbon whiskey also combine attractively with espresso. Espresso fortified with grappa is probably the most classic of these combinations; Italians sometimes call it *Caffè*

Corretto. Many people add a dollop of sweet liqueur to straight espresso after dinner in place of the usual sugar, thus both sweetening and flavoring the cup. In fact, some enthusiasts do a sort of coffee overload by making the liqueur a dark-roast, coffee-based liqueur like Kahlua. This combination (or intensification) of coffee on coffee is a bit much to my taste, but those who find that the palace of culinary wisdom lies along the road of excess may enjoy it.

Of course the purist will protest that you shouldn't mix good brandy or liqueur and good espresso but should enjoy them separately, side by side. However, in a culture where caffè latte is flavored with chocolate mint syrup, such objections seem a bit hypothetical.

Recipes for Fortified Espresso Drinks

Here are a few recipes that straightforwardly combine spirits and espresso, or at least make use of the unique capabilities of the espresso machine. Aside from the *San Francisco Cappuccino*, they are all my own inventions, and usually represent traditional coffee-and-spirits recipes reinterpreted for the espresso cuisine.

San Francisco Cappuccino is a traditional yet curiously named drink, since it uses no espresso at all but is a combination of hot chocolate, brandy, and frothed milk. Once a favorite of Italian-Americans and their Bohemian associates in San Francisco, it has now virtually disappeared except at some old-time San Francisco bars like the wonderful Tosca in the North Beach neighborhood, where these drinks are still assembled using a pair of 60-year-old Victoria Arduino espresso machines.

To make the San Francisco Cappuccino at home, start by making a hot chocolate concentrate by dissolving about 1 rounded teaspoon of unsweetened chocolate powder in a ½-ounce or so of hot water in a 6-ounce, stemmed glass of the heavy, flared variety designed for Irish Coffee. The spoon must remain in the glass throughout the assembling of the drink, since it absorbs the heat of the hot liquids and prevents the glass from cracking. Top the chocolate concentrate with about 3 ounces of hot frothed milk, or enough to fill the glass about ⅔ full. Add 1 jigger (1½ ounces) of brandy; sweeten lightly if you prefer; mix and serve.

For **Espresso Gloria** (my name for a drink based on the traditional recipe for Coffee Gloria) combine 1 serving (1½ ounces) of freshly brewed espresso, about 3 ounces of hot water, 1 jigger of brandy, and granulated or brown sugar to taste (1 teaspoonful is traditional). Follow the same recipe, substituting Calvados, or apple brandy, for the grape brandy, and this drink becomes Espresso Normandy. To make it taste even more like northern France, use a darker roast coffee than usual (the nearly black style that is usually sold as Dark French) when brewing the espresso.

Espresso Royal follows the recipe for Espresso Gloria but flames the brandy. Combine 1 serving (1½ ounces) of freshly brewed espresso and about 3 ounces of hot water. Partly dissolve 1 sugar cube in a warmed silver spoon of brandy. Hold the spoon over the espresso/water mixture and ignite the brandy. Contemplate the effect, then stir into the coffee.

Many traditional coffee drinks add a head of lightly

whipped cream to sweetened, fortified coffee. In the United States the most famous of these drinks is *Irish Coffee*, a drink popular in the 1950s through 1970s. A good variation on the whipped cream, spirits, and coffee theme for the espresso lover might be called *Venetian Espresso*, after the similarly named and constructed traditional drink, *Venetian Coffee*.

For **Venetian Espresso** place a demitasse spoon and sugar to taste (one rounded teaspoon is traditional) in an Irish Coffee glass. The spoon must remain in the glass while the coffee is poured. Brew 1 medium-to-long serving (2 to 2 ½ ounces) of espresso per glass, and pour over the sugar. Add 1 jigger of brandy and stir. Remove the spoon and top with whipping cream that has been beaten until it is partly stiff but still pours. The whipping cream should be soft enough to float with an even line on the surface of the coffee, rather than bob around in lumps. If the cream tends to sink or mix with the coffee, pour it into a teaspoon held just at the surface of the coffee. This drink should not be stirred; sip the hot coffee and brandy through the cool whipped cream. Made with crème de cacao, this drink could plausibly be called *Espresso Cacao*. Other spirits also taste good: bourbon, rum, Strega, Calvados, grappa, and almost any liqueur, including (for espresso overload lovers) dark-roast coffee liqueurs like Kahlua.

Espresso Brûlot Diabolique, Espresso Brûlot, Espresso Diable, and **Espresso Flambé** are all plausible names for a theatrical drink in which a flavored brandy mixture is heated, ignited, and combined with espresso. For each cup assemble 1 serving (1½ ounces) of freshly brewed espresso, about 2 ounces of hot water, 1½ jiggers of brandy, granulated or brown sugar to taste (1 teaspoonful is traditional), 1 large strip orange peel, 1 small strip lemon peel, and 10 whole cloves.

Warm the sugar, brandy, cloves, and orange and lemon peels in a chafing dish. Stir gently to dissolve the sugar. Place 1 serving espresso and 2 ounces hot water in each cup or glass, and place around the chafing dish. When the brandy mixture has been gently warmed (you should be able to smell the brandy very clearly from 3 feet away if it's ready), pass a lighted match over the chafing dish. The brandy should ignite. If it doesn't, it probably is not warm enough. Let the brandy burn for as long as you get a reaction from your audience (but not over half a minute), then ladle over the coffee. The flame will usually die when the brandy is ladled into the glasses. Don't let the brandy burn too long, or the flame will consume all of the alcohol.

If you don't have a chafing dish, put the sugar in each glass before you add the coffee; heat the brandy, cloves, and citrus peel on the stove. When the fumes are rising, pour into a fancy bowl and bring to the table. Carefully lay an ounce or two of the brandy mixture atop each glass of coffee; if you pour the brandy gently, it will float on the surface of the coffee. To ignite the brandy, pass a match over each glass; to douse the flame, mix the brandy and coffee.

If you have trouble getting the brandy to float, try holding a teaspoon on the surface of the coffee and pouring the brandy mixture onto the spoon, letting it spread from there over the coffee. Also remember to add the sugar to the coffee, not to the brandy mixture, or the sugar will make the brandy too heavy to float. If you're serving only one or two cups, you can simply heat the brandy mixture right in the ladle.

The same drink is good made with dark rum. Follow the preceding instructions, substituting rum for brandy and omitting the flaming process. Another possibility is to use half rum and half brandy.

MAKING ESPRESSO-BASED LIQUEURS AT HOME

Styles of coffee liqueurs differ. Espresso lovers are apt to prefer those heavy-bodied versions based on dark-roasted coffee, like the famous Kahlua, and the recipes I give below follow that style. If you prefer a lighter-bodied liqueur, like those commercial products based on Kona coffees, for example, reduce the amount of glycerin or omit it entirely, and use a lighter roast of coffee: a light French or Viennese roast, for example. No matter what you do, your liqueur will never taste quite like the commercial products, but you may end up liking your version better. Store your liqueur in tightly capped bottles in the refrigerator.

To make your liqueur you will need I part freshly brewed espresso, I part brown sugar, I part 90 to I00 proof vodka, I inch fresh vanilla bean per cup vodka, and, if you want your liqueur to reflect the heavy body of commercial products, I teaspoon glycerin per cup vodka.

Slit the vanilla bean. Brew the espresso, and immedi-

ately, while the espresso is still hot, add the vanilla bean and sugar. Stir until the sugar is dissolved, then add the vodka and (if you wish a heavy-bodied drink) the glycerine. Refrigerate in a sterilized, capped bottle. After a few days taste; when you begin to detect the vanilla flavor, discard the vanilla bean and store the liqueur in a second sterilized bottle, or pour and serve. If you're impatient, substitute vanilla extract for the bean; add 2 or 3 drops per cup of vodka any time after you've brewed the espresso. Variations: Substitute dark rum or brandy for the vodka, or add a dash of tequila to every cup of rum or vodka.

The simple addition of chocolate turns espresso liqueur into *Mocha Liqueur*. Make a chocolate concentrate by thoroughly combining in a double boiler one ounce of unsweetened baking chocolate and ½ cup boiling water. Add ½ tablespoon, more or less to taste, of this mixture to every cup of the finished coffee liqueur before refrigerating, mixing thoroughly. The chocolate may separate when the liqueur is stored; invert the bottle and shake gently before serving.

The addition of cream turns espresso liqueur into *Liqueur Caffè Latte*, or Mocha liqueur into *Liqueur Mocha Latte*. Add the cream (the ultra-pasteurized kind with a long shelf life) after the liqueur is finished and you have extracted the vanilla bean. To every cup of liqueur add I tablespoon cream, more or less to taste. Mix thoroughly and store in capped, sterilized bottles in the refrigerator. This dairy-fortified liqueur will keep for about a month. Invert the bottle and gently shake before serving.

ESPRESSO PLACES

Espresso Break

Caffeine, the Doctors, and Espresso

Recently I was sitting in downtown Seattle over an empty cappuccino cup near one of the city's many espresso carts. This particular cart was nestled under the marquee of the Coliseum Theater, a landmark movie palace from the early days of cinema now closed and waiting for someone with money to turn it into boutiques. The cart is owned by Chuck Beek, one of the entrepreneurs credited with getting Seattle's extraordinarily successful espresso cart business underway.

UNDER THE COLISEUM MARQUEE

An espresso cart, in the unlikely case you haven't seen one, is a sort of mobile espresso bar, an espresso bar on wheels, complete with machine, grinder, a small refrigerator, and the rest of the gear needed to produce espresso cuisine, all neatly built into a cart compact enough for one or two people to roll out of seclusion every morning into some promising urban setting filled with passing potential espresso buyers. An innovator named Craig Donarum built Seattle's first espresso cart in 1980 and sold it to Chuck Beek some months later. From that one cart hundreds more have sprung, to the point that there is hardly a large filling station or supermarket in the Seattle area without an espresso cart in front of it, dispensing Italian coffees to passing shoppers and motorists.

Chuck's current cart (the original is reverently preserved back inside the Coliseum Theater among boxes of drink cups, plastic spoons, and napkins) is surrounded by a few tables and chairs, some T-shirts and postcards, and Chuck's neon sign, which simply reads "Caffeine" ("Truth in advertising," Chuck says). On the morning I describe three or four people were lined up at the cart buying caffè lattes to take back to work, some exchanging neighborhood and workplace gossip with Chuck. The tables were occupied by people doing the time-honored things people do while drinking coffee: One man was reading a newspaper, several well-dressed women were holding an animated conversation (I later learned they worked at the nearby Nordstrom department store), others were conducting business, and I was sitting as I have for so many hours of my life, examining the world from over my recently emptied cappuccino cup and thinking.

FROM CAIRO TO ESPRESSO CART

In this case, my thoughts revolved around the very earliest coffee sellers in history, those entrepreneurs who first took coffee beyond the confines of Muslim Sufi meetings in early sixteenth-century Cairo and began selling it in the streets to the public, creating the first "coffeehouses" in history, and beginning coffee's extraordinary rise to beverage of choice for over half the world. These informal, open-air establishments (probably more coffee stands or kiosks than "houses" at first) must in many ways have resembled Chuck Beek's cart under the Coliseum Theater marquee in Seattle. One gets the impression from the illustrations that accompany nineteenth-century European travelers' accounts, for example, that the less formal "coffeehouses" of Muslim tradition were simple, open-air pavilions or kiosks that, like Chuck Beek's operation, simply slipped into unused urban spaces and allowed their seating arrangements to spill casually out into the streets. The customers sitting at the tables in these illustrations look to be occupying themselves in much the same way as those of us sitting under the Coliseum Theater marquee: some quietly talking; others alone, lost in thought, observing the passing scene, or reading; but all representing aspects of the peculiar sort of semi-intellectual loafing—reading, talking, writing, playing chess, staring into space and thinking—typical of coffeehouses, cafés, and caffès throughout history.

Resistance to Improvised Institutions

It is even possible to see a parallel between the resistance these early coffeehouses suffered from religious and secular authorities and the (albeit much milder) resistance the Seattle espresso carts suffered in their "early" history (10 or 12 years ago!), when they were hounded by municipal authorities for lacking approved equipment and permits, etc. In both cases rather humble urban entrepreneurs and their coffee-hungry clientele managed in the end to triumph over the resistance of authorities to the irregularities presented by such improvised institutions. And in both cases one can sense the liveliness and humanity such operations bring to the urban scene, the way the simple presence of a cart selling coffee and a few tables and chairs can transform a corner that (in the case of Chuck Beek's operation) might otherwise be deserted, inhabited only by scraps of newspaper and a few weeds poking out of the sidewalk. An espresso machine and a few tables and chairs instantly create a place where one can *be* rather than simply pass through.

There is an even more humble archetype of public coffee selling that has an equally long history: The coffee vendor, the lone man (or woman) with a pot of coffee, a few cups, and a stool, who wanders the streets and sets up wherever somebody slows down long enough to crave a cup of coffee. References to such humble entrepreneurs abound in the published history of coffee. An eighteenth-century illustration of a Near Eastern coffee vendor is reproduced on page 158. I hardly expected to encounter similar ultimately shoestring entrepreneurs in the 1990s but given the unemployment rate

Throughout its history coffee has been sold by strolling street vendors, who in effect bring the coffeehouse to the customer. This vendor, as depicted in an early eighteenth-century French travel book, looks obviously undercapitalized but is nevertheless elegant in gesture and clearly confident of his product.

and the popularity of espresso drinks, I should have known better. All someone had to do was update the archetype for the automobile age. While waiting in a cab in a toll line in Boston in 1993, I saw a robust young man striding between the stopped cars, a sort of insulated

tank on his back, a cup dispenser on his belt, and a sign on his chest advertising "Caffè Latte," serving hot coffee and consolation through car windows to frustrated motorists.

Careful Design vs. Casual Serendipity

The capacity for a modest, self-contained espresso-selling operation to transform a dead space that people simply walk through on their way to somewhere else into a lively arena for human interaction and contemplation has, of course, not gone unnoticed by planners, architects, and building owners. Just across the street from Chuck Beek's espresso cart and the Coliseum Theater is a Starbucks espresso kiosk, situated in the glossy lobby of the City Centre building.

Although the Starbucks organization started small and continues to exhibit a coffee fanatic's passion for quality, it nevertheless is an operation in most ways antithetical to Chuck Beek's: large; sleek if not slick in its handling of marketing, graphics and architecture; and traded on stock exchanges. That contrast in style and scale is displayed here: the Starbucks kiosk is splendidly designed and exquisitely situated among indoor plants and marble, the result of careful design rather than casual serendipity like Chuck's location across the street. Nevertheless, the continuity with the first coffeehouses and kiosks in sixteenth century Cairo continues to be striking: again, a public space, in this case impressive but impersonal, filled with benches that only an architect could love, is transformed into a space where people talk, read, or contemplate, at least briefly, over their cappuccino or "latte."

A PECULIAR STYLE OF MENTAL RECREATION

It remains an open question whether the particular brand of intellectual loafing associated with the coffeehouse from its inception—reading, talking, chess playing, and staring into space and thinking—is directly related to the special kind of mental intoxication peculiar to coffee and caffeine (I believe that it is), or whether the character of the coffeehouse, once established, simply maintained itself for other cultural reasons. What is certain is that as coffee spread through the world, so did the coffeehouse and its peculiar style of mental recreation. From Cairo it was carried to Syria, from Syria to Turkish Constantinople, from Turkey to Venice via trade, and to Vienna via the failed Turkish siege of that city in 1683. From Venice and Vienna the habit of coffee and coffeehouses spread to the rest of Western Europe, and from there to North America.

(continued on page 164)

Coffeehouses along a river in Damascus, as depicted in an early nineteenth-century engraving. The informality of the arrangements in these places mirrors a similar informality in today's impromptu street cafés created by espresso carts and stands.

| | |

ESPRESSO BREAK

CAFFEINE, THE DOCTORS, AND ESPRESSO

Why Coffee?

Even bringing up health in a book on espresso may strike some readers as contradictory. Although coffee first appeared in human culture as a medicine, the kind we now patronize as "herbal," the modern medical establishment has viewed coffee over the years with suspicion, so much so that coffee has become one of the most intensely scrutinized of modern foods and beverages.

Why has the medical establishment chosen to focus so much attention on coffee in particular? Why not on scores of other foods, from white mushrooms to black pepper to spinach, all of which have been accused of promoting various diseases? Perhaps because coffee is such an appealing dietary scapegoat. Since it has no nutritive value and makes us feel good for no reason, coffee may end up higher on the medical hit list than other foods or beverages that may offer equal or greater grounds for suspicion, but are more nourishing and less fun.

Furthermore, since in its dark, syrupy richness espresso seems an intensification of the very idea of coffee, some readers also may worry that espresso represents an intensification of coffee's purported health risks.

For Now, Sip Easy

For now, however, the espresso lover can rest easy, or at least sip easy. Despite studying coffee intensively for over fifteen years, medical science has yet to prove any definite connection between moderate caffeine or coffee consumption and disease or birth defects. For every study that tentatively suggests a relationship between moderate coffee drinking and some disease, or between moderate coffee drinking during pregnancy and a pattern of birth defects, other studies—usually involving larger test populations or more stringent controls—are published that contradict the earlier, critical studies. It is safe to say that the medical profession is farther away than ever from nailing coffee with the kind of warning labels that decorate wine and beer bottles, despite continued intensive testing and study.

Nor do espresso drinkers appear to be at any greater risk than their filter-coffee-drinking colleagues. Although scientific studies of the impact of coffee on health seldom isolate variables like brewing method and style of roast, nothing in the literature so far would indicate that any characteristic specific to espresso poses special health risks, aside from the fact that it tastes so good we may be tempted to drink too much of it.

In fact, there even may be some basis for arguing that espresso is healthier, or at least less unhealthy, than the ordinary thin-bodied stuff found in restaurant carafes. The darker roasts used in the espresso cuisine contain somewhat less caffeine than lighter-roasted coffees, and considerably less of the components that contribute to the acidic sensation some people associate with their stomach problems.

However, such speculation is irresponsible at this point. Until the researchers begin to take into account brewing method, style of roast, and serving customs in their investigations, not only will we know nothing verifiable about the differences between espresso and filter coffee in terms of impact on health, but we probably won't know much about the health impact of coffee generally.

Any Conclusions?

Despite all of the uncertainties, is there anything the health-conscious espresso lover should conclude from the evidence gathered so far? The following, I would argue:

1) If you are a moderate espresso drinker (i.e., if you don't regularly indulge in doubles and triples and are capable of waiting a couple of

"Coffee Comes to the Aid of the Muse", a nineteenth-century painting, illustrates in poetic terms the short-term advantages of coffee for the creative endeavor.

hours between servings), and are in good health, then you should relax and enjoy. Nothing has been proven against temperate coffee or espresso drinking, and for the near future at least, it appears that nothing will be.

On the other hand:

2) Make certain your espresso drinking *is* moderate. The studies that appear to exonerate coffee drinking are not exonerating the habits of mindless coffeeholics who drink ten cups a day out of the office carafe, or espresso fanatics who pour down triple lattes or double espressos at every coffee break. What is being exonerated is "moderate" intake of caffeine, usually defined as 300 to 500 milligrams per day, or the equivalent of three to five cups of American-style drip coffee (assuming one is not also consuming caffeinated colas or over-the-counter medicines containing caffeine).

Unfortunately, it is not clear how much caffeine a single serving of espresso packs, since espresso brewing procedures differ so widely. A *properly* concentrated, properly pressed two-ounce serving of espresso probably contains around the same 100 to 150 milligrams of caffeine that the average cup of filter coffee does. So, following the definition of moderation in coffee drinking given above, you could consume three to four such proper servings of espresso per day and still remain safely in the "moderate" category. However, the misplaced generosity of many North American espresso operators places such estimates in question, since these inexperienced zealots tend to continue pressing caffeine and bitter chemicals out of the ground coffee long after the flavor oils have been extracted. If you care about your caffeine intake and love espresso, learn to brew it yourself or patronize places that understand the espresso cuisine and press the coffee properly.

3) If you are pregnant or have certain health conditions, you should bring your coffee-drinking habit to the attention of your physician, even if it is a moderate habit. Aside from pregnancy, health conditions that merit examining your coffee drinking include benign breast lumps, high cholesterol, heart disease, and some digestive complaints. Again, *nothing has been proven against moderate coffee consumption* in any of these situations, but some physicians may disagree with the studies, or new studies may have appeared that complicate the matter.

Finally, and above all:

4) Enjoy rather than swill. In the espresso cuisine good health and good aesthetics go hand in hand. The Italian practice of stopping frequently during the day to concentrate on the brief but repeated pleasure of a single *small* serving of espresso is probably considerably healthier than the North American practice of carrying off triple lattes or double cappuccinos to work. Espresso drinkers who learn to appreciate the perfection of a single, correctly pressed serving of espresso or the few fragrant ounces of a classic cappuccino, and who take the time to give themselves over to the experience of that perfection, to the *moment* of the coffee, to its warmth and perfume, are far less likely to abuse caffeine than are those coffee drinkers who carry around Styrofoam cups of dead office coffee or half-cold caffè latte all day.

For a discussion of caffeine-free coffees turn to pages 63–68. I discuss caffeine-free coffees and coffee and health issues at greater length in my book *Coffee: A Guide to Buying, Brewing, and Enjoying.*

ESPRESSO REDEFINES THE AMERICAN COFFEE PLACE

The first American coffeehouses were modeled on those in England but in many cases appear to have been more taverns and inns than coffeehouses in either the Muslim or the modern sense. How these early tavern-coffeehouses evolved into the array of coffee-drinking establishments familiar to North Americans of the 1950s (the coffee shop of vinyl booths and bottomless cup, the diner, the roadside café and truck stop) is not clear. But what is clear is that espresso, arriving from Italy in the 1930s through 1950s, has redefined the North American coffeehouse and café.

Espresso from its inception was a public phenomenon, involving the application of technology to coffee-making on a scale difficult to duplicate at home (at least until recently). It permitted the production of a coffee so technically superior to the simpler coffees Italians brewed at home that it added a technical reason to the social reasons for taking one's coffee in public. Not only was it more fun to get one's coffee in a bar or caffè, but with the advent of espresso the coffee tasted better than coffee brewed at home, and embodied a certain mystique or glamour as well.

From Club to Caffè

Espresso appears to have been introduced into North American life by Italian immigrants, who established informal social clubs, places where men from the Italian-American community met to drink coffee from the recently popularized espresso machines, play cards, talk, and cut business deals. The transformation of these social clubs into public caffès, where the Italians were joined and often displaced by the writers, artists, and intellectuals who found a sympathetic atmosphere in Italian-American neighborhoods, was a gradual development, and one that in some places still continues.

For example, one of the more fashionable places to take a cappuccino in San Francisco during the late 1980s was a small, plain Italian cigar-store-cum-caffè, which, like so many similar places before it, was in the process of changing from neighborhood hangout for local Italians to destination for in-the-know artists, writers, and professionals. On the other, earlier end of the chronology, the first American espresso caffè that I have a date for is Caffè Reggio in New York's Greenwich Village. The Caffè Reggio was founded as a social club in 1927, but by the 1950s, when I first visited it, it had been pretty much converted to an artists' and writers' hangout. Caffè Reggio is still in business, by the way. The original espresso machine has been retired to icon status in one corner, but the 1930s Little Italy, garage-sale-baroque furniture and bric-a-brac interior continues splendidly intact.

Espresso Goes to College

By the 1950s Italian-Americans were opening caffès that from their inception catered to a mix of patrons, both Italian-Americans and a local mélange of writers, artists, and similar types. Many of these postwar establishments were situated in university communities, like the Caffè

Mediterraneum in Berkeley (opened in 1958). I clearly recall the mid-1960s crowd in the Mediterraneum, which typically combined students, a few faculty, some older intellectuals whose main function in life seemed to be sitting at the same table every day and discussing the news, various brands of radicals, from early Black Power advocates to orthodox Marxists to sentimental Trotskyists, and a table of Italian locals from the neighborhood, including the mailman and the barber from next door.

Today college communities continue to support a growing espresso caffè culture, as American students discover what their French counterparts have known for centuries: that studying at a marble-top table over a cappuccino beats the library every time. The commitment of student communities to espresso often can be fierce and rather exclusive; the editor of this book reports walking into a large caffè near the University of California at Berkeley and asking for coffee. "We don't serve *coffee*," growled the barman in response. "We only serve *espresso*."

MUSIC AND SUBVERSION

Patrons at early Near Eastern coffeehouses didn't solely read, talk, and contemplate, however. They also listened to music, watched puppet shows, and listened to storytellers and other performers. "Generally in the coffeehouses there are many violins, flute players, and musicians, who are hired by the proprietor of the coffeehouse to play and sing much of the day, with the end of drawing in customers," wrote Jean de Thévenot in his seventeenth-century account of Turkish coffeehouses.

There was also considerable concern among political authorities regarding the nature of the talk that went on at sixteenth- and seventeenth-century coffeehouses, both in the Near East and in Europe. With so many people spending so many hours comparing notes on the events of the day, might not the conclusions they reached be dangerous to the current political and social order? This fear more than any other probably lay behind the numerous early efforts to suppress coffeehouses. Charles II of England, for example, in his short-lived suppression of coffeehouses in 1675, contended that "in such houses . . . divers false, malitious and scandalous reports are devised and spread abroad to the Defamation of His Majestie's Government, and to the Disturbance of the Peace and Quiet of the Realm."

Monarchical Misgivings

Events in the eighteenth century seemed to confirm such monarchical misgivings. Coffee and coffeehouses were credited with roles in both the French and American revolutions, as well as in the Enlightenment, the period in Western thought that planted the seeds of those revolutions. The famous Parisian Café de Procope was the regular haunt of Enlightenment thinkers like Voltaire and Condorcet, and Camille Desmoulins's speech at the Café Foy is said to have set off the first overtly rebellious act of the French Revolution, the storming of the Bastille. Across the Atlantic, Boston's famous coffeehouse, the Green Dragon, was called, in an often-cited description by Daniel Webster, "the headquarters of the Revolution."

THE COUNTERCULTURE ARCHETYPE

Such potentially subversive carryings on, combined with the long-established coffeehouse custom of offering small-scale, informal entertainment, connects most clearly with still another North American archetype of the public dispensing of espresso, the counterculture coffeehouse, the candle-in-a-bottle, poster-on-the-wall informal night-club of the rebels, poets, beats, and folk and jazz lovers of the 1950s. Such places, which in the 1950s often appeared in the same neighborhoods as the Italian-American social-clubs-turned-espresso-caffès mentioned earlier, were usually opened by artist-musician-writer types to cater to the same. They put less emphasis on espresso, reading, and contemplation than their Italian-American counterparts, and a bit more on music, performance, and wine and beer.

The counterculture coffeehouse appeared on its way out during the sleek 1980s, but it is now making a robust comeback in urban pockets all over the country, from Los Angeles to Seattle, where, had I risen from my table under the Coliseum Theater marquee that day some months ago and walked south a few blocks, I could have taken an excellent espresso at classic coffeehouses like The Crocodile, where by day a sleepy restfulness prevails, while one feels the casual artist funk of the decor waiting for nightfall and the arrival of the first musicians and performers.

Intimacy and Experiment

Coffeehouses provided and still provide a range of cultural possibility that is virtually unique in our society: They function as the usual coffee-culture hangouts for reading, talking, and contemplation; as art galleries free of the taste-making controls of commercial galleries; as informal nightclubs free of the taste-making controls of the commercial music industry; and as places where artists and performers as diverse as poets, standup comedians, magicians, political satirists, and belly dancers can entertain their particular small but passionate audiences, nurturing an aesthetic culture based on face-to-face intimacy and experiment rather than passive consuming, media, and spectacle.

It is difficult to say how important espresso in particular, and coffee generally, is to the gestalt of the counterculture coffeehouse, since beer and wine usually also are consumed there. But the historical association of coffeehouses with a sort of alternate aesthetic culture (a culture occasionally deemed subversive or dangerous by authorities) suggests that the particular mental intoxication of coffee, a sort of individualistic mental reverie, promotes a different kind of cultural stance and a different kind of art, than the more diffused, often soggier and more collective euphoria of alcohol. If so, coffee and the espresso machine are central to the maverick contribution that the counterculture coffeehouse has made and continues to make to North American aesthetic culture.

THE SPECIALTY COFFEE CONTRIBUTION

The last strand of recent coffee history to contribute to contemporary espresso culture is what is often called specialty coffee, a phenomenon that, like the Italian-American caffè and the counterculture coffeehouse, was born (or reborn) in the 1950s and has been gaining momentum ever since. The specialty coffee store is, of course, the place where one buys, in bulk, usually amid brown-stained wood and burlap-bag decor, coffees with names like Ethiopian Harrar or Sumatran Lintong, or (if the store owner is not a purist) Chocolate-Mint or Irish Creme.

These stores are based on the nineteenth- and early twentieth-century tradition of small stores that roasted their own coffee in a little machine behind the counter and sold it directly to the public in bulk, custom-ground. A few specialty stores are direct survivors from that period, but most are the brainchildren of pioneering entrepreneurs who recreated the tradition with skill and passion. As the quality of mass-distributed, canned coffee declined in the 1960s and 1970s owing to the substitution of bland, cheap robusta coffee for higher-quality arabica coffees, the specialty coffee business picked up steam, first in university towns and gentrified urban pockets, then in city centers and suburban malls. From a few coffee-loving idealists scratching a living from behind pine

London youths stimulate themselves at one of the some 2,000 espresso bars that dotted Great Britain during the British espresso bar craze of the post-World-War-II period. No doubt a Vespa or Lambretta waited just outside the door. By the 1970s it was hard to find an espresso in Great Britain, though a revival is now underway.

counters, the specialty coffee world has grown to become a powerful alternative to the commercial coffee business, with a specialty coffee trade association, publications, meetings, and other trappings of an established niche-occupier in modern commerce.

Caffès Despite Themselves

Espresso was not central to the interests of the early pioneers of specialty coffee, who preferred to devote themselves to delicious subtleties like the differences between Ethiopian Harrar and Ethiopian Yirgacheffe, or to the nuances of house blends. Nevertheless, as specialty coffee stores began to accommodate their customers by adding tables, chairs, and pastries, dispensing espresso also became an important part of their business. The expanding Starbucks chain, which I mentioned earlier, started as a classic specialty coffee business but appears to be more and more turning into a chain of high-quality espresso bars. The Coffee Connection chain in Boston began as a specialty store in Cambridge's Harvard Square, and the Coffee Connection store there still functions as a meeting place and caffè for the university community.

Even speciality stores that do their best to avoid becoming caffè-ified, like the famous, resolutely purist Peet's chain in the San Francisco Bay Area, have been turned by their admirers, willy-nilly, into improvised standup coffeebars. I recall driving through North Berkeley, seeing a crowd ahead of me milling around at the edge of the street, and thinking that perhaps a disaster had occurred. Then I realized that the people were all holding coffee cups and that I simply had happened upon the morning crowd at the local Peet's store. Such, once more, is the civilizing function of coffee—it can turn even a curb and a piece of dirty sidewalk into a place to talk and be.

FINDING ESPRESSO COFFEE AND EQUIPMENT

I discuss sources for espresso coffees in Chapter 6, pages 84–85. Coffee specialty stores can usually be found in the yellow pages under the "Coffee Dealer, Retail" heading.

Some categories of espresso equipment are easier to find than others. Caffettiere (category 1, pages 108–109), small electric steam-pressure countertop brewers (category 3, page 110), and the more modest pump machines (category 4, pages 111–112) are now stocked in most upscale department stores, and even carried by some chain discount stores. For those in isolated rural areas, good cookware catalogs usually carry a similar fundamental range of equipment.

Specialized espresso grinders, larger pump machines and automatic machines, and manual piston machines (category 5, pages 113–114) usually can be obtained only in well-stocked specialty coffee stores or through the mail from such stores.

Finally, some kinds of equipment—home roasting apparatus, stovetop brewers with frothing function (category 2, page 109), grain mills, knock-out boxes and milk thermometers, and the more exotic piston machines—are difficult to find no matter where you shop or how many catalogs you subscribe to.

If you cannot find sources for any of the following categories of home equipment and wish to order them through the mail, please write to me care of the publisher at the address on the copyright page and request information on one or more of the following:

- specialized espresso grinders and larger pump machines;
- home roasting apparatus and green beans;
- home manual piston machines;
- bar accessories (knock-out boxes, milk thermometers, frothing pitchers, specialized spoons and receptacles), stovetop brewers with frothing function, and manual coffee grinders and grain mills suitable for espresso cuisine.

Espresso Magazines

Two lively voices of North American espresso culture, *Café Olé* and *Fresh Cup* magazines, display advertisements for everything from espresso garnishes to T-shirts and update their readers on specialty coffee news. Their addresses:

Café Olé
Wordsmith Publishing
115 Bell Street
Seattle, Washington 98121
206/443-1156

Fresh Cup
Fresh Cup Publishing Co.
P.O. Box 82817
Portland, Oregon 97282-0817
503/224-8544
FAX 503/653-5690

Advice on Espresso as Business

Those readers contemplating entering the coffee or espresso business and who are seeking advice should plan to attend the annual meeting and show of the Specialty Coffee Association of America, usually held in May. The association can be reached at One World Trade Center, Suite 800, Long Beach, California 90831-0800, 310/983-8090, FAX 310/983-8091.

PHOTO AND ILLUSTRATION CREDITS

A'Roma Roasters & Coffee House, Santa Rosa, Calif.,
pages 53, 86

Baldwin, Rebecca Lee, illustration by Rebecca Baldwin for
T-shirts and mugs by Fabric Art, Inc., Portland,
Ore., page 35

BE-MA Editrice, Milan, Italy: Ambrogio Fumagalli's
Macchine da Caffè, pages 11, 17 (both), 18 (top),
19 (detail), 30 (both), 31 (top and center), 105

Brasilia s.r.l., Padia, Italy, and Rosito & Bisani, Inc., Los
Angeles, page 121

Braun, Inc., Lynnfield, Mass., pages 32 (bottom),
101 (top), 136 (center)

Caffé Acorto Incorporated, Bellevue, Wash.,
page 20 (bottom)

Cimbali SpA, Milan, Italy, page 18 (bottom)

Davids, Kenneth, pages 1, 33 (top)

DeLonghi America, Carlstadt, N.J., page 112

FAEMA, S.p.A., Milan, Italy, and Gary Valenti, Inc.,
Maspeth, N.Y., page 19 (left)

Hulton Deutsch Collection, London, England, page 167

KRUPS North America, Inc., Closter, N.J., pages 110
(top), 136 (top)

Mosuki, Ltd./La Victoria Arduino, New York., pages v, 9,
156

Nuova Simonelli, Belforte del Chienti, Italy, and Nuova
Distribution Centre Inc., Vancouver, B.C., Canada,
page 20 (top)

Peerless Coffee Co., Oakland, Calif., George and Sonja
Vukasin, owners, page 93

Pinacoteca di Brera, Milan, Italy, page 23

Robert Bosch Corporation, Broadview, Ill., page 101
(bottom)

Saeco U.S.A., Inc., Saddle Brook, N.J., page 33 (bottom),
103, 136 (bottom)

Tea & Coffee Trade Journal, New York: William Ukers' *All
About Coffee*, pages 12, 49, 54, 58 (all), 59, 61, 72,
83, 155, 158, 159, 161

Thomas Cara family collection, San Francisco, Calif., pages
31 (bottom), 32 (top)

UNIC S.A., Nice, France, page 95

Zassenhaus GmbH & Co., Germany, and Windward
Trading Co., San Rafael, Calif., page 102

CHAPTER OPENING ILLUSTRATIONS

Preface, page v: The excitement of early espresso culture captured in a 1922 Victoria Arduino poster: power, speed, sophistication, modernity; fast trains and espresso-powered people.

Chapter 1, page 1: This older Venetian coffee sign suggests that all of the imagined dark romance of Africa was available to those Italians of the period who chose to purchase a cup of Poggi coffee. Most Italian coffee was imported from Africa, as it still is.

Chapter 2, page 9: A gondola-load of Victoria Arduino espresso machines in early twentieth-century Venice. The sheer quantity of shiny new machines in one place at one time suggests how rapidly espresso culture spread through Italy during the years preceding World War I.

Chapter 3, page 35: One of many witty celebrations of espresso culture currently decorating the torsos of North Americans. From a T-shirt design by Rebecca Lee Baldwin for Fabric Art, Inc., Portland, Oregon.

Chapter 4, page 49: An open-air coffee-roasting stand from early twentieth-century Spain, before roast-and-ground canned coffees started the world on its steep slide to coffee mediocrity.

Chapter 5, page 59: Early eighteenth-century illustration of coffee branch, flowers, and fruit from Jean de La Roque's *Voyage de l'Arabie Heureuse.*

Chapter 6, page 83: On a Costa Rican coffee farm early in this century, water carries coffee fruit from fields to a central processing facility. This photograph gives a good notion of the relatively small scale of commercial *Coffea arabica* trees.

Chapter 7, page 95: This extraordinary device, designed by one Mario Levi and first manufactured in 1919, combines roasting, grinding, and brewing processes in a single apparatus. Only about fifty of these machines were manufactured, and none is known to have survived.

Chapter 8, page 105: This device from 1930s Italy woke its owner to a demitasse of freshly brewed espresso. At the appointed time the clock activated the electric element in the little caffettiera in the center of the device; when steam pressure in the caffettiera had forced enough fresh espresso into the cup at the right to trigger a balance mechanism, the alarm sounded.

Chapter 9, page 121: Two golden streams of perfect crema.

Chapter 10, page 155: Tourists and accommodating waiter pose in front of Venice's Caffè Florian in the 1920s. The quintessence of touristic caffè romanticism.

INDEX

Kenneth Davids

Although Kenneth Davids admits to having devoted a good part of his earlier years to sitting in cafés drinking someone else's espresso, his formal involvement with coffee began in the early 1970s when he opened his own coffeehouse in Berkeley, California. In 1976 he published *Coffee: A Guide to Buying, Brewing, and Enjoying,* one of the earliest contemporary books on the subject and now one of the most respected. *Coffee* is now in its fourth edition and has sold well over 150,000 copies.

Born in Chicago, Davids graduated from Northwestern University and later received his master's degree in litera- ture from the University of California at Berkeley. He has lived in Europe, Mexico, and Hawaii, his travels including several weeks spent among coffee roasters and fanciers in Great Britain preparing a British edition of his general book on coffee, and a stay in Italy in preparation for *Espresso: Ultimate Coffee.* In addition to writing on coffee, he has published a novel and translations. He is currently a member of the Educational and Promotional Materials Committee of the Specialty Coffee Association of America. He teaches writing and history at California College of Arts and Crafts and resides in Piedmont, California.